What?

Experiments for the young scientist

Robert W. Wood
Illustrated by Steve Hoeft

TAB Books

Division of McGraw-Hill, Inc.

New York   San Francisco   Washington, D.C.   Auckland   Bogotá
Caracas   Lisbon   London   Madrid   Mexico City   Milan
Montreal   New Delhi   San Juan   Singapore
Sydney   Tokyo   Toronto

© 1994 by **Robert W. Wood**.
Published by TAB Books, a division of McGraw-Hill, Inc.

pbk 1 2 3 4 5 6 7 8 9 0 DOH/DOH 9 9 8 7 6 5 4

Library of Congress Cataloging-in-Publication Data

Wood, Robert W., 1933–
    What? : experiments for the young scientist / by Robert W. Wood;
  illustrations by Steve Hoeft.
      p.   cm.
    Includes index.
    ISBN 0-07-051636-7
    1. Science—Experiments—Juvenile literature.   2. Science-
  -Experiments—Popular works.   [1. Science—Experiments.
    2. Experiments.]   I. Hoeft, Steve, ill.   II. Title.
    Q164.W67   1994
    507.8—dc20   94-3086
                                                                       CIP
                                                                        AC

Acquisitions editor: Kimberly Tabor
Editorial team: Steven Bolt, Editor
                Susan W. Kagey, Managing Editor
                Joanne Slike, Executive Editor
                Joann Woy, Indexer
Production team: Katherine G. Brown, Director
                Rhonda E. Baker, Coding
                Jan Fisher, Desktop Operator
                Nancy K. Mickley, Proofreading
                Brenda S. Wilhide, Computer Illustrator
Design team: Jaclyn J. Boone, Designer
                Brian Allison, Associate Designer
Cover photograph: Brent Blair, Harrisburg, Pa.   0516367
Cover copy writer: Cathy Mentzer   KIDS

Contents

Introduction   vii

Symbols used in this book   ix

THE YOUNG ENGINEER

1   What makes an airplane fly?   3

2   What is reduced air pressure?   8

3   What makes a rocket go?   11

4   What are gears for?   16

5   What are pulleys for?   19

6   What is an electrical circuit?   24

7   What are magnetic fields?   28

8   What is electromagnetism?   33

THE YOUNG ASTRONOMER

9   What makes a star twinkle?   39

10   What keeps the North Star from moving?   43

11   What is your horizon?   46

12   What is your latitude?   49

13   What is your meridian?   51

THE YOUNG CHEMIST

14   What are acids and bases?   57

15   What makes ice float?   62

16   What is starch?   65

17   What is carbon?   69

18   What is carbon dioxide?   72

19   What is water?   75

THE YOUNG METEOROLOGIST

20   What are clouds?   80

21   What are rain, snow, and hail?   83

22   What is the Coriolis force?   87

23   What are highs, lows, and fronts?   90

24   What is the dew point?   93

25   What is a rainbow?   96

THE YOUNG BIOLOGIST

26   What is photosynthesis?   101

27   What do rings in a tree show?   105

28   What are lungs for?   108

29   What does our heart do?   112

THE YOUNG PHYSICIST

30   What is surface tension?   119

31   What does air weigh?   121

32   What are sound waves?   124

33   What bends light?   127

34   What causes volcanoes to erupt?   131

Index   137

About the author   149

Introduction

Science began thousands of years before anyone learned to write. We'll never know who discovered fire, who invented the wheel, or who first tried to explain what the sun is and where it went each night. In general, mathematics and engineering, followed by the physical sciences and biology, were probably the first of the sciences to be developed.

As individuals, we don't always solve problems in a systematic fashion. We can decide, however, to use several steps in a scientific method to explain problems and their solutions.

1. Ask a question or state a problem. For example, is there a connection between rain and dew?
2. Form the hypothesis or a possible explanation. In the preceding example, you know that dew and rain are both water, and that on cool mornings fog can leave dew on the ground. This can lead you to believe that there is a connection between the moisture in the air and falling temperatures.
3. Experiment. In this case, you could hold a pan of ice cubes over a pot of hot water and observe the results. You probably would see a mist form over the pot of water and drops form on the bottom of the pan.
4. Interpret data and form a conclusion. From the experiment, you would know that rain and dew both come from the air when moisture condenses from a cooling temperature.

This book is part of a series of books that ask such stimulating questions as *Why?*, *What?*, *When?*, *Who?*, and *Where?* science happens. Each book is divided into six parts; each part relates to a different science. You should know, however, that sciences tend to overlap from one field to another. Astronomers need to know something about physics and biologists need an understanding of chemistry, and so on.

Each part of this book consists of easy experiments—that begin by asking a question—followed by the materials list, a step-by-step procedure, and then the results. At the end of each experiment, you will find suggestions for further studies that will broaden the scope of the experiment. Science trivia and oddities have been included for your amusement.

Symbols
used in this book

 adult supervision

 scissors

 sharp objects

 safety goggles

 fire

 electricity

 stove

Part 1
The young engineer

Engineering is a combination of art and science. Engineers apply scientific knowledge to use power and materials in practical ways. Engineers are responsible for the design and construction of dams, highways, and skyscrapers as well as airplanes, cars, and other forms of transportation.

Amazing engineering projects from the past include the Panama Canal, the Pyramids of Egypt, and the San Francisco-Oakland Bay Bridge. Engineers design projects, select materials, and calculate the strength of structures to make sure the structures will stand up under the worst conditions they might encounter.

Engineering includes many different fields that often overlap. For example, an aeronautical engineer designs the shape and structure of an aircraft, but also needs to be knowledgeable of the type of engines that power the aircraft and the hydraulic systems that operate the controls. A mechanical engineer works with the design of machines, the strength of materials, and the use of gears and levers to accomplish work.

Through the science of engineering we have increased our comfort, safety, and overall lifestyles.

Pyramids of Egypt

San Francisco-Oakland Bay Bridge

1
What makes an airplane fly?

materials ☆
- ❏ Sheet of paper
- ❏ Scissors
- ❏ Transparent tape
- ❏ Pencil
- ❏ Electric fan

procedure ☆
1. Remembering to always cut away from yourself, cut a strip of paper about 3 inches wide and about 11 inches long (8 cm × 28 cm).

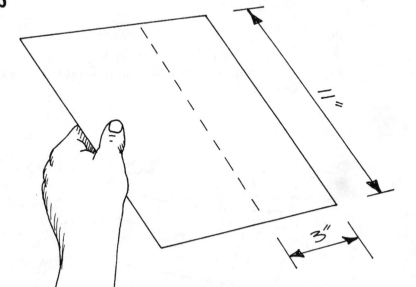

Fold the paper in half.

2. Fold the paper in half (3 × 5½ inches) (8 cm × 14 cm). Do not crease the fold. With the ends together, slide one side of the folded paper so that it is about ½ inch (1.3 cm) shorter than the other and fasten it in place with tape. One side of the folded paper should be flat while the other side is slightly curved. You now have a paper airfoil designed like the wing on an airplane.

The top of the paper should be curved slightly.

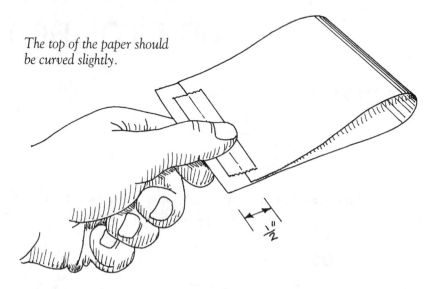

3. Place the pencil inside the loop at the folded end and hold the wing with the curved side up in front of the fan. What does the wing do?

Your airfoil should try to lift.

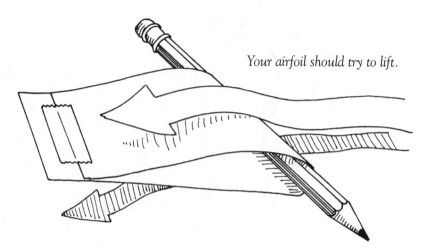

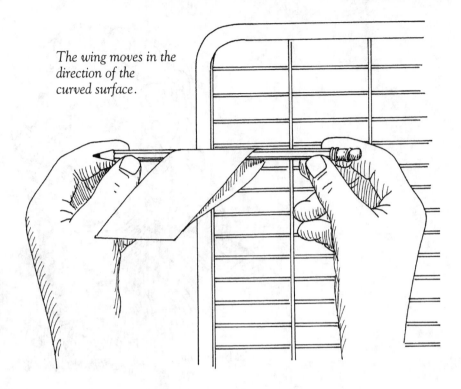

The wing moves in the direction of the curved surface.

4. Turn the wing upside down and try it again. Now what happens?

results ☆ In the 1700s, a Swiss mathematician named Daniel Bernoulli discovered that the pressure of air is lowered as the speed of the air increases. When the *airstream* approaches the front of the wing, some of the air travels under the wing in a straight line. The other air moves over the top of the wing. The air moving over the top is forced to make a longer trip to get to the back edge of the wing. The air over the top must arrive at the back of the wing at the same time as the air moving under the wing.

Because of the extra distance, the air across the top must race to catch up. This increased speed over the top of the wing reduces the air pressure above the wing. The air pressure under the wing remains the same. The difference in pressure causes the wing to lift.

When you hold the wing in front of your fan with the curved side up, the wing wants to rise. But when the wing is held upside down

Daniel Bernoulli

in front of your fan, the wing tries to move down. Both times it moves to the curved side; the curved side creates lift.

further ☆ studies Now that you understand how a curved surface can create lift, notice the shape of propellers on small airplanes and helicopters. Propellers create thrust and lift the same way that wings do.

did you ☆ know?
- ❑ That the biggest problem the Wright brothers had was not the design of their airplane but building an engine light enough to provide the necessary power.
- ❑ That the first design for a helicopter was found in the notebooks of Leonardo da Vinci.
- ❑ That the wings on a space shuttle don't provide any lift while the shuttle is in space.
- ❑ That gliders (sailplanes) can stay aloft for hours because of the lift provided by their extra-long wings.

Orville and Wilbur Wright

2
What is reduced air pressure?

materials ☆
- ❏ Small funnel
- ❏ Candle
- ❏ Metal jar lid
- ❏ Match

procedure ☆

1. With the help of an adult, light the candle, drop a few drops of wax into the jar lid, and stand the candle in the lid. Place the candle on a worktable or kitchen counter.

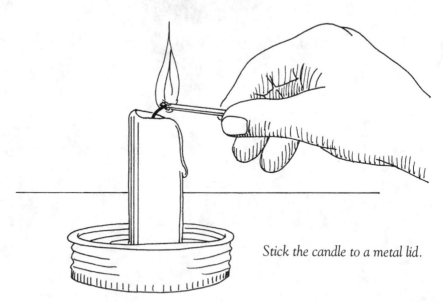

Stick the candle to a metal lid.

2. Try to blow out the flame by blowing through the small end of the funnel. What happens?
3. Now turn the funnel around and try to blow out the flame through the large end of the funnel. Did the candle go out?

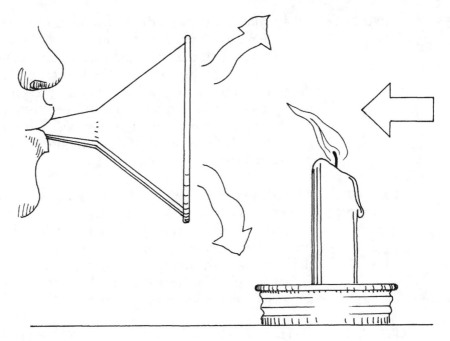

The air pressure near the funnel is lower.

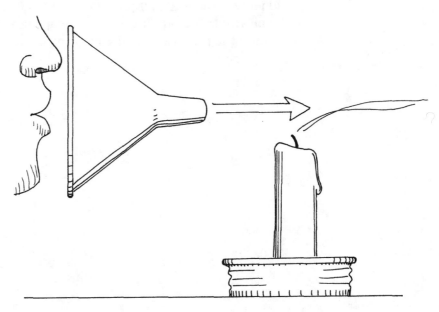

The air pressure is strong enough to blow out the flame.

results ☆ When you blew through the small end, the airstream traveled from the narrow part of the funnel through the larger area where it spread out. When the air spread out, the air pressure in the opening of the funnel lowered. The lowered air pressure caused the surrounding air, which was at normal pressure, to move toward the open end of the funnel. The flame bent toward the open end of the funnel, making it hard to blow out. When you blew through the large end of the funnel, the air pressure was not reduced, and you easily blew out the flame.

further studies ☆ To further study the effects of air pressure, ask an adult for permission to plug the hose of a tank-type vacuum cleaner into the exhaust end and connect it to the small end of a funnel. Now turn on the vacuum and place a Ping-Pong ball in the funnel. Will the ball stay in the funnel if you turn it upside down? Remove the funnel and support the ball on a column of air. How far can you tilt the column of air before the ball falls?

did you know? ☆
❑ That surface winds can blow toward an approaching storm because of the lower air pressure in the storm.
❑ That tornadoes cause buildings to explode because of the differences in air pressure. When the whirling air of a tornado suddenly reduces the air pressure on the outside of a building, the air inside the building cannot escape fast enough to equalize the pressure, and the building explodes.

3
What makes
a rocket go?

materials ☆
- ❏ Large plastic bottle
- ❏ Cork that fits the plastic bottle
- ❏ Bicycle tire pump inflating needle (used for footballs, basketballs, etc.)
- ❏ Cardboard
- ❏ Tape
- ❏ Nail
- ❏ Funnel
- ❏ Water

procedure ☆

1. Remembering to always cut away from yourself, cut and shape four cardboard fins for the rocket. Fasten the fins to the plastic bottle with tape.

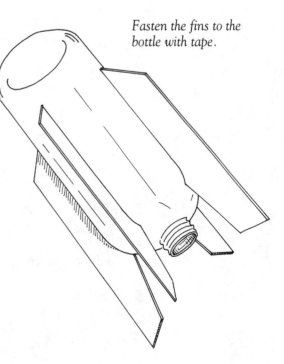

Fasten the fins to the bottle with tape.

2. Place the cork on a piece of scrap wood and use the nail to make a small hole in the cork for a tight fit for the inflating needle.

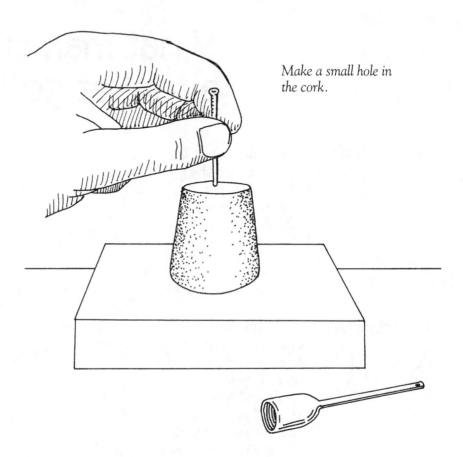

Make a small hole in the cork.

3. Fill the bottle about one-fourth full of water and push the cork into the bottle top.
4. Take the rocket to the middle of a vacant field. Attach the needle to the tire pump, and insert the needle in the hole in the cork.
5. Stand the rocket on its fins, stretch out the tire pump hose so that you can stand clear of the rocket, and start pumping.

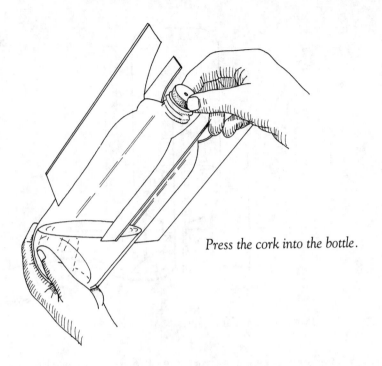

Press the cork into the bottle.

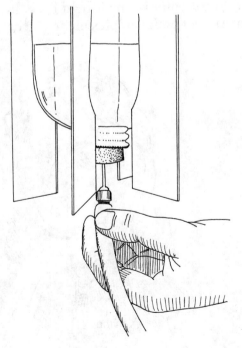

*Push the needle
into the hole.*

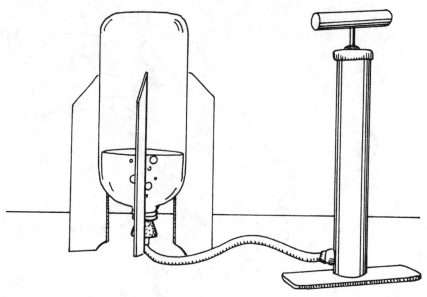

Pump air into the rocket.

results ☆ Isaac Newton's third law of motion states that for every action, there is an equal but opposite reaction. If you push or pull anything, it pushes or pulls right back. In your experiment, the pumping causes the air pressure in the bottle rocket to build up

Isaac Newton

until the cork can't hold the pressure. The cork pops from the bottle and releases the water pushed by compressed air. The rocket is pushed in the opposite direction and into the air. The action is the water and compressed air being forced from the rocket. The reaction is the rocket being pushed in the opposite direction. Rockets burn fuel that expands and forces hot gases from nozzles, pushing the rocket into the air.

further ☆ studies
Experiment with different amounts of water in your rocket. Record the results to see how much water is needed to produce the best performance. Place the end of a garden hose in a clear area and turn the water on full. Do you notice an action and a reaction?

did you ☆ know?
❑ That the Chinese used rockets in warfare more than 700 years ago.
❑ That in the War of 1812, the British used solid-fuel rockets during the siege of Fort McHenry. It was this siege that inspired Francis Scott Key to write the phrase "the rockets' red glare" in "The Star-Spangled Banner."

4
What are gears for?

materials ☆
- ❏ Three bottle caps with crimped edges
- ❏ Three small nails
- ❏ Hammer
- ❏ Wooden board

procedure ☆ 1. Make sure the bottle caps are round and not bent. Have an adult help you fasten a bottle cap to the board by driving a nail through the center of one cap. Don't drive in the nail too far because the cap must be free to turn.

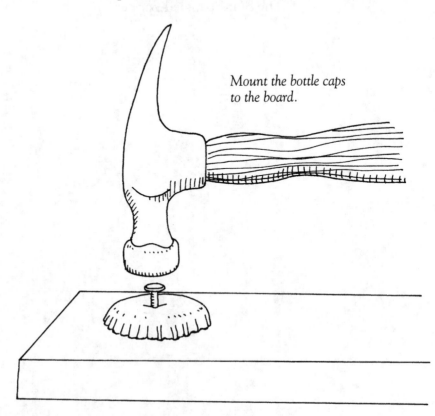

Mount the bottle caps to the board.

2. Next, place another cap directly alongside the first one and fasten it the same way. Mount the third cap next to second cap with the remaining nail. All caps must be adjacent to each other but free to turn. Now turn one of the end caps with your finger.

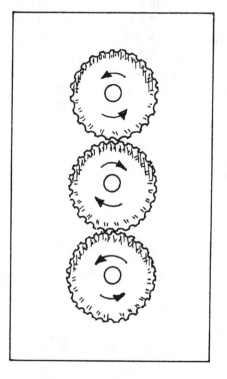

The gears turn in opposite directions.

results ☆ When you turn any one of the caps, the other caps turn in opposite directions. The points on the caps act like teeth on gears. The teeth from one gear mesh with the teeth on another gear so that when one turns it turns another, but in the opposite direction. So you can see that gears are used to change the direction of a *force*. Another advantage of gears is that when a small gear is used with a larger gear, the force and speed of the gears can be changed. Further, gears with angled teeth can be used together to change the direction of a force to any angle. Cars use these types of gears to transfer power from the engine to the drive wheels.

further ☆ Examine a bicycle. Even if it doesn't have gears that shift, you can
studies see that the pedals are attached to a large gear that uses a chain to
transfer power to a smaller gear on the back wheel.

did you ☆ ❑ That if the gear with the pedals was half as big as the gear on
know? the wheel, the speed of the wheel would be cut in half, but the
power to the wheel would be doubled. This type of
arrangement can be used for starting off or going up hills.
Bicycles with several gears use these types of gears.
❑ That in early civilizations, gears were connected to water
wheels to capture the force of falling water and change the
direction of this force to do work.

5
What are pulleys for?

materials ☆
- ❏ Stiff wire from coat hanger
- ❏ Two spools from sewing thread
- ❏ String
- ❏ Pliers
- ❏ Wire cutters
- ❏ Scissors
- ❏ Weight (such as a heavy bolt)

procedure ☆

1. Use wire cutters to cut a piece of wire, and then thread the wire through one of the spools. Now bend the ends of the wire up and hook them together to complete the pulley. Cut another piece of wire and make another pulley from the second spool.

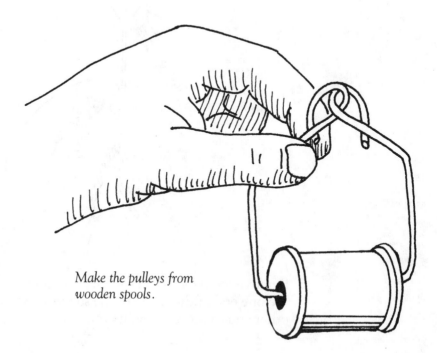

Make the pulleys from wooden spools.

2. Fasten one of the pulleys to a support as shown and feed the string through the pulley. Tie the weight to one end of the string and pull down on the other end. You have made a *fixed pulley*.

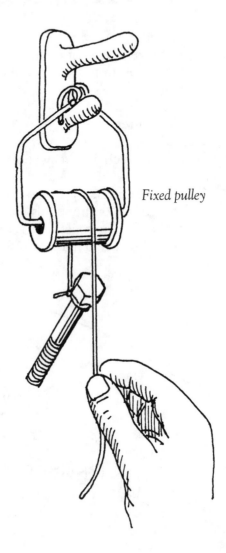

Fixed pulley

3. Remove the pulley from the support and tie it to the weight. Tie one end of the string to the support and pull up on the other end to lift the weight. You have made a *movable pulley*.

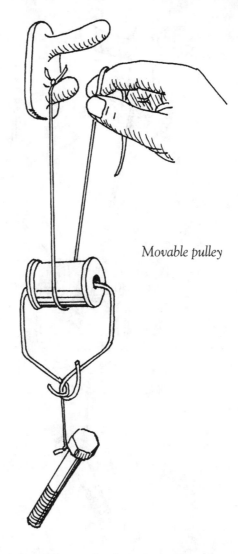

Movable pulley

4. With the weight still attached to the pulley, fasten the second pulley to a support near the first support. Thread the free end of the string through the second pulley and pull down on the string to lift the weight. Now you have made a *single block and tackle*.

results ☆ *Mechanical advantage* is a rating given to a device that compares the ratio of the output force to the input force necessary to do work. A single fixed pulley has no mechanical advantage to lift the weight. The only advantage is that you can pull from a more convenient direction and add your body weight to the force of the

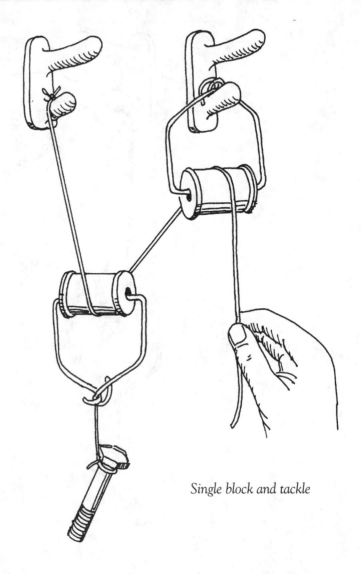

Single block and tackle

pull. With a movable pulley, where the pulley is attached to the weight, you pull up to lift the weight but the mechanical advantage is 2. The force needed to lift the weight is half that of a fixed pulley. In other words, a 2-pound force can lift 4 pounds. When you use a block and tackle, the mechanical advantage is still 2, but now you can pull down and add your weight to the force of the pull.

further ☆ studies

Notice the next time you pass a flag pole whether a pulley is used to raise the flag. Look at a picture of a sail boat. Can you find any pulleys? If you see a crane lifting something, you should see several pulleys working together to lift the weight.

did you ☆ know?

❑ That if you loop the string through the pulleys a second time, making four lifting strings, it would be a *double block and tackle* and the mechanical advantage would be 4. The ability to do work increases with the number of pulleys and ropes that are used.

❑ That, as mechanical advantage increases, the distance the weight is moved decreases by the same amount. With a fixed pulley, the weight moves the same distance as the pull. When the mechanical advantage is 2, the weight moves half the distance for the same length of pull.

6
What is an
electrical circuit?

materials ☆
- ❑ 1½-volt flashlight battery
- ❑ 1½-volt flashlight bulb
- ❑ Bell-type wire about 12 inches (30.5 cm) long

procedure ☆

1. Be sure to wear safety goggles throughout this experiment. Have an adult carefully strip the insulation from both ends of the wire for you. Now wrap one of the bare ends tightly around the metal base of the bulb.

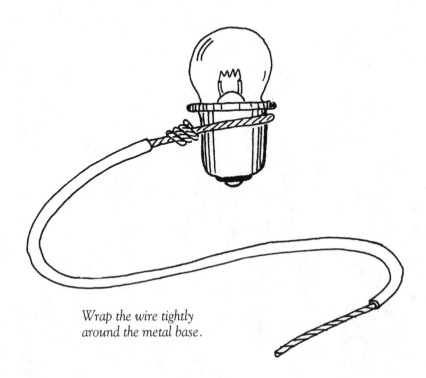

*Wrap the wire tightly
around the metal base.*

2. Stand the battery upright on a table with the bottom of the battery resting on the other end of the wire.

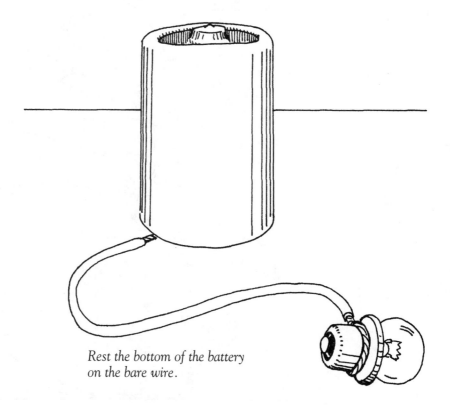

Rest the bottom of the battery on the bare wire.

3. Look at the bottom of the bulb. You will see a small metal mound surrounded by dark plastic. Press this point to the raised center on top of the battery.

results ☆ In order for an *electrical circuit* to work, it must be a complete path from the source of power through the *load* (the energy receiver) and back to the source (the battery). In this experiment, the bottom of the battery—the negative end—is the source. The current flows from the battery, through the wire, to the metal side of the bulb. The little wire inside the bulb is called the *filament*. The filament is connected to the metal on the side and the metal tip on the bottom of the bulb. The current travels through the filament, out the bottom of the bulb, and back to the battery.

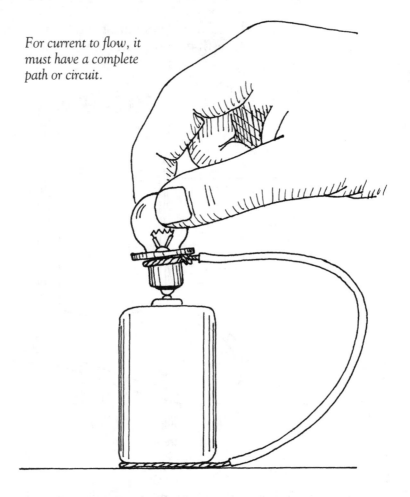

For current to flow, it must have a complete path or circuit.

If there is a break in any part of the circuit, the current can't flow. When you touched the bulb to the battery, the circuit was complete, current flowed, and the bulb burned. When you use a battery, the current is called *direct current* (dc). With direct current, the current flows only in one direction. When a generator is used, such as the huge generators that supply power to our homes, the current is called *alternating current* (ac). With alternating current, the current travels first in one direction, then the other. In both cases, the circuit must be complete for current to flow.

**further ☆
studies** Count the number of appliances (lamps, ceiling lights, radios, etc.) in just one room in your home. Do all of the appliances work? Are

they complete circuits when the switch is off? Ask an adult how many circuits you have in the service entrance panel in your home. What are the circuit breakers used for inside the panel?

did you ☆
know?

❑ That the most common light bulb in your home is called an *incandescent light* and that the first practical light bulb was invented by Thomas Edison in 1879.

❑ That 90 percent of the energy used to light an incandescent bulb is wasted in heat.

❑ That George Westinghouse and Nikola Tesla put on a dazzling display at the 1893 Chicago Exposition that included 90,000 lamps, a model kitchen with an electric coffee pot, and a grill with a heated saucepan and chafing dish. They used twelve 1,000-horsepower, 2,300-volt generators and almost a half million feet of wire.

Thomas Edison

Nikola Tesla

7
What are
magnetic fields?

materials ☆
- ❏ Magnet
- ❏ Steel needle
- ❏ Fine thread about 8 inches (20.3 cm) long
- ❏ Pencil
- ❏ Drinking glass
- ❏ Paper about 1 × 2 inches (2.5 × 5.0 cm)

procedure ☆   1. Magnetize the needle by stroking it about 20 times across one end of the magnet.

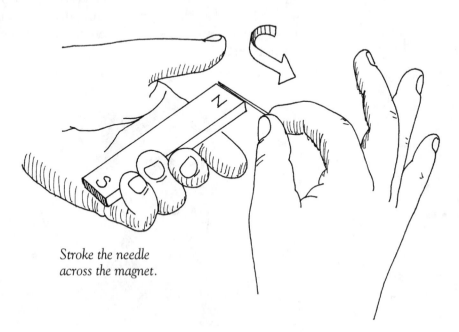

Stroke the needle across the magnet.

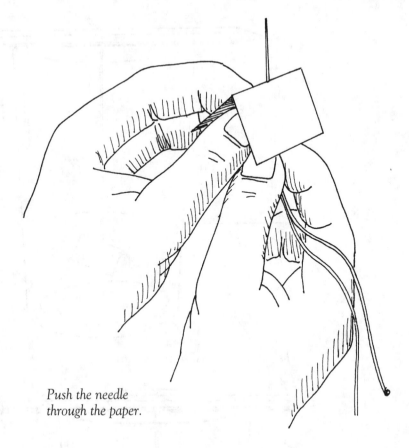

*Push the needle
through the paper.*

2. Thread the needle and tie a knot in one end of the thread. Leave the other end of the thread free so that it can be pulled through the paper. Fold the paper in the middle to make a 1-inch (2.54 cm) square. Now spread the paper a little and push the needle through the center from the inside of the fold. Gently pull the thread through the paper so that the knot is not pulled through. Remove the needle from the free end of the thread.

3. Tie the free end of the thread around the middle of the pencil. The length of thread should suspend the paper about an inch (2.54 cm) above the bottom of the glass.

4. Spread the paper tentlike and insert the needle horizontally through the center of both sides of the paper. Lower the needle inside the glass so that it is suspended by the thread and pencil. The needle must be free to turn.

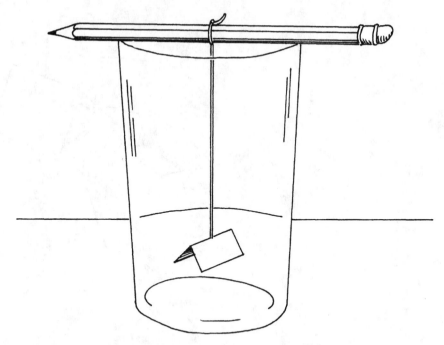

The paper tent must be free to turn.

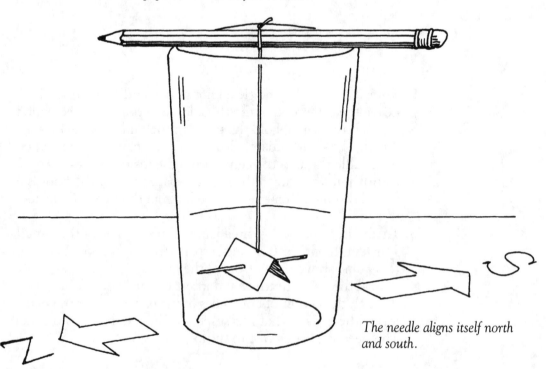

The needle aligns itself north and south.

results ☆ In 1600, William Gilbert, a physician to Queen Elizabeth I, published his discovery that the earth is a huge magnet. One *magnetic pole* is near the earth's North Pole, the other near the earth's South Pole. A *magnetic field* is made up of lines of force that travel in a circular pattern from one pole to the other. At the northern and southern magnetic poles, the magnetic lines of force are vertical. Halfway between the poles, near the equator, the lines are horizontal.

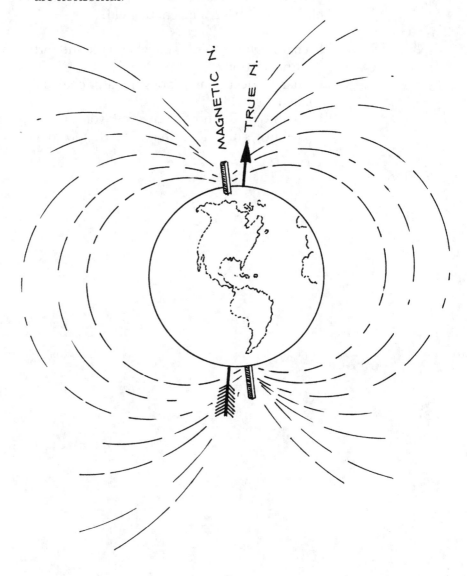

In the experiment, first the needle turns a few times, and then aligns itself north and south with the lines of force in the earth's magnetic field. When an electrical current flows along a wire, the current generates its own magnetic field that surrounds the wire.

further ☆ studies Place a magnetic compass near a wire connected to a battery. Does the compass needle move? When passing under power lines with a radio on an AM station, can you hear the static of a magnetic field? Do we live in a magnetic field?

did you ☆ know?
- ❑ That migrating birds and whales use the earth's magnetic field for navigation.
- ❑ That an electric motor or generator could not work without a magnetic field.
- ❑ That no matter how many times you cut a magnet in half, it will always have a north and south pole for each piece.

8
What is electromagnetism?

materials ☆
- ❏ ¼-inch (6.35 mm) bolt about 3 inches (7.6 cm) long
- ❏ ¼-inch (6.35 mm) nut and 2 washers
- ❏ 6-volt lantern battery
- ❏ Small, insulated copper wire about three feet (.914 meters) long

procedure ☆

1. Wear safety goggles throughout this experiment. Slide one of the washers onto the bolt. Leave several inches of wire to connect to the battery and wrap about 50 turns of wire snugly around the bolt. Leave several inches of wire at this end for the other connection to the battery.

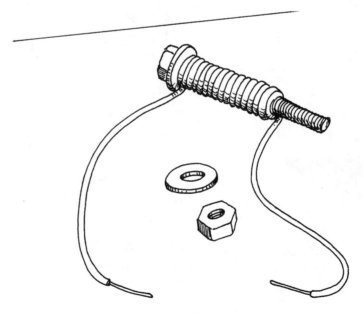

Wrap the wire tightly around the bolt.

2. Slide the remaining washer onto the bolt and screw the nut in place. Have an adult strip about ½ inch (1.3 cm) of the insulation from each of the free ends of the wire. Connect the bare ends to each terminal on the battery. You now have an *electromagnet*.

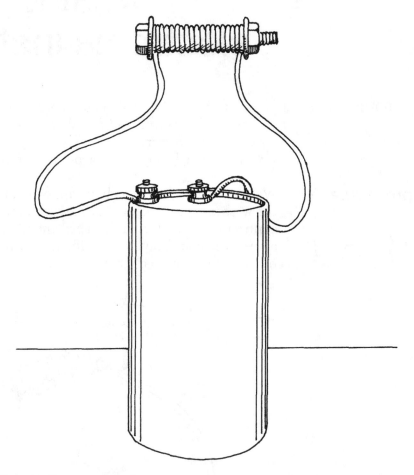

Connect the wires to the battery.

 3. Touch the magnet to a few small nails or paper clips. Disconnect one wire from the battery and try again.

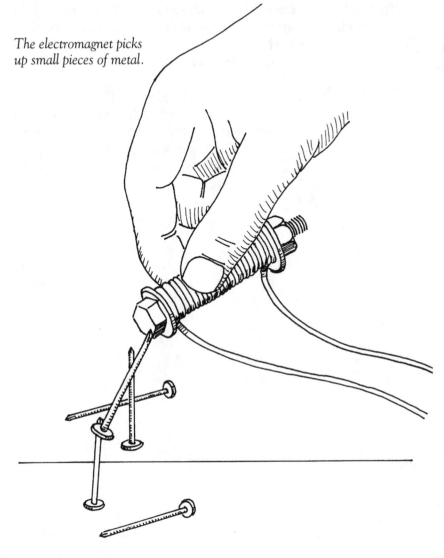

The electromagnet picks up small pieces of metal.

results ☆ The magnet was able to pick up small pieces of metal as long as the wires were connected to the battery. *Electromagnetism* is magnetism produced by an electric current. When an electric current flows through a wire, it produces a magnetic field around the wire. If the wire is wound into coils around a piece of iron, the magnetic field is increased enough so that it can pick up small pieces of metal.

further ☆ Increase the number of turns of wire around the bolt. Does the
studies magnetic field increase? Can the magnetic field pick up brass?
Aluminum? Copper? How is an electromagnet different from a
permanent magnet?

did you ☆ ❏ That in winter of 1819–20, Hans Christian Oersted discovered
know? electromagnetism when he found that an electric current
flowing through a wire would cause a compass needle to move.
❏ That the starter in a car is activated by an electromagnet.
❏ That huge electromagnets are used with cranes to move iron
and steel.

Part 2
The young astronomer

Astronomy is the exciting study of the universe. It is probably one of the oldest sciences. The earliest cave dwellers gazed at the sky and wondered what they saw. At night, they noticed how the stars rose in the east, how they moved slowly across a giant dome, and how they then sank below the western horizon.

When some tribes began to plant crops, they needed to know when to plant and when to harvest. This need led to the development of *solar calendars* based on the movements of the sun during the year. Even today, our clocks are regulated by the precise measurements of the movements of heavenly bodies.

Hundreds of years ago people believed that the earth was at the center of the universe and the sun, moon, and stars moved around the earth once every day. Today, we know that the earth is a planet that moves around the sun. The sun is a star and our star system, or *galaxy*, has about 100,000 million stars. The largest telescopes show thousands of millions of these galaxies. Each galaxy contains thousands of millions of stars, and almost all of them are moving away from us. The universe is expanding.

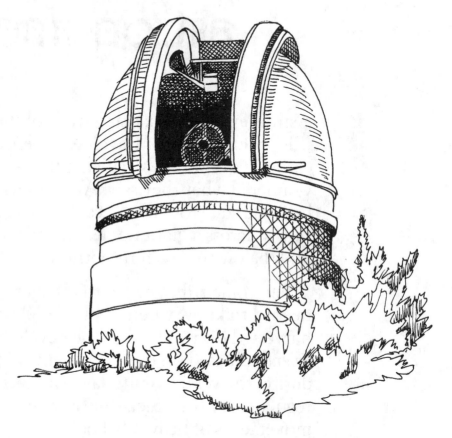

The *solar system* is made up of the sun and the planets and other heavenly bodies that revolve around the sun. Our system is part of a giant galaxy called the *Milky Way*. Our knowledge of the universe is constantly growing through advances made in astronomy. You can easily see how astronomy is an important field for the future exploration of space.

9
What makes
a star twinkle?

materials ☆
- ❑ Small nail
- ❑ Empty cereal box
- ❑ Flashlight
- ❑ Table
- ❑ Dark room
- ❑ Electric hot plate or stove

procedure ☆
1. With an adult's help, use the nail to make a few small holes on one side of the cereal box.
2. Turn on the flashlight and place it in the box so that the light shines toward the holes.
3. Close the flaps on the box so that no light escapes except through the holes.
4. Place the box at one end of the table with the holes facing the other end. Ask an adult to place the hot plate in the middle of the table. First, make sure the cord is out of the way, then turn on the hot plate, and turn out the lights. Once the hot plate is turned on, be careful not to touch the heated plate.
5. Move to the end of the table and look at the lights from the box through the warm air rising from the hot plate.

results ☆ Heating air causes the air to become less dense. Because the warm air rising from the hot plate moves up with varying temperatures, it has a variety of densities. As a beam of light travels from one density to another, it bends slightly. Because the density is constantly changing, the lights from the box appear to twinkle. The earth's atmosphere moves in a similar manner with constantly varying temperatures and densities. The movement of the layers of atmosphere bend and scatter starlight so that stars

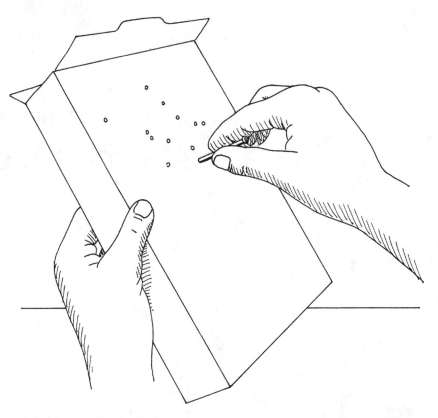

Punch a few small holes in the box.

seem to twinkle. In space, without the atmosphere, stars do not twinkle.

further ☆ studies
Place a pencil or a straw in a glass of water. Notice how the pencil appears to be broken at the waterline. This optical illusion is caused by the bending of light waves through the different densities of the air and the water. This bending is called *refraction*. Is a mirage caused by refraction?

did you ☆ know?
❑ That when you are traveling down a highway in the summer and you see what appears to be a pool of water in the distance, what you actually see is a mirage caused by the hot air near the surface of the pavement.
❑ That the term *mirage* comes from the Latin word, *mirare*, meaning "to look at."

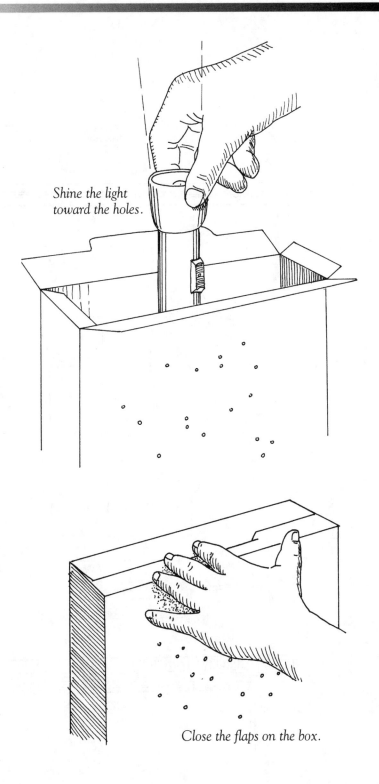

Shine the light toward the holes.

Close the flaps on the box.

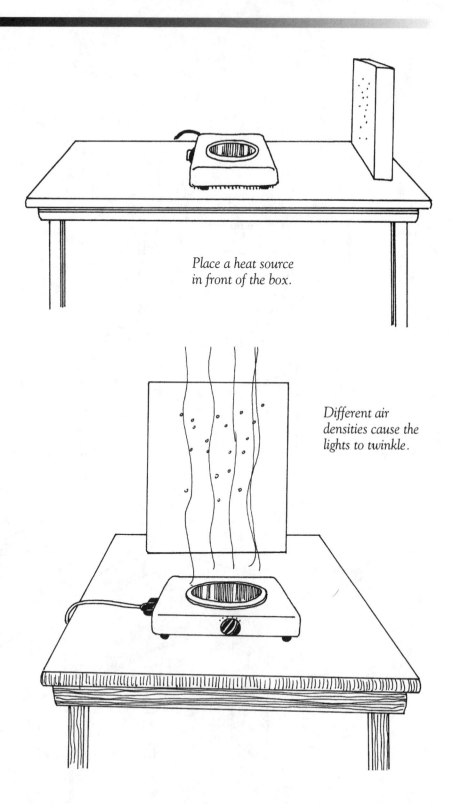

*Place a heat source
in front of the box.*

*Different air
densities cause the
lights to twinkle.*

10
What keeps the North Star from moving?

materials ☆
- ❑ Clear night
- ❑ Map showing the constellations in the northern sky
- ❑ Camera with an adjustable shutter speed
- ❑ Tripod or solid platform
- ❑ Black-and-white film

procedure ☆

1. Locate the Big Dipper and Little Dipper in the northern sky. On winter evenings, the Little Dipper is to the left of the Big Dipper and has its handle pointing up. At this time, the Big Dipper has its handle pointing down. On summer evenings, the positions are reversed. Now find the North Star (sometimes called the *polestar*). The two stars in the front of the Big Dipper are called the two pointer stars. Count about five spaces (one space equals the distance between the pointer stars) in a straight line toward the Little Dipper. The North Star is the end star in the handle of the Little Dipper.

2. Ask an adult for permission to use a 35mm camera. Also, ask for assistance in loading the black-and-white film into the camera and help in mounting the camera on a tripod. Have an adult help you if you are not familiar with setting the camera shutter speed so that the film has a long (30 minutes to an hour) exposure time.

3. Center the North Star in the view finder and take the picture. It is very important to keep the camera steady during the exposure. Use a cable release if you have one. Take several pictures, increasing the time for each exposure.

results ☆ When the film is developed, you should see star trails curving around the actual pole of the sky. The movement is caused by the rotation of the earth. The North Star appears to be stationary because it is directly over the axis on which the earth spins.

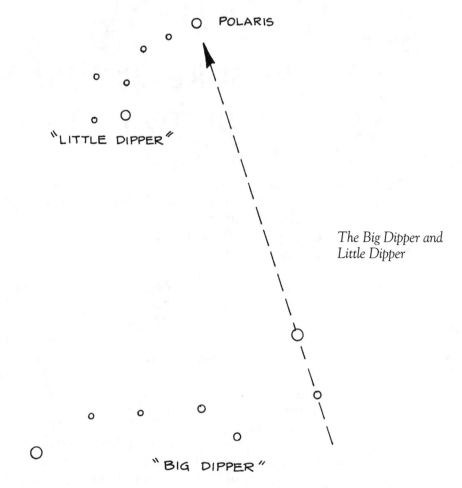

O POLARIS

"LITTLE DIPPER"

The Big Dipper and
Little Dipper

"BIG DIPPER"

further ☆   The Little Dipper can be seen from the northern hemisphere, but
studies   what constellation has stars pointing to the South Pole of the sky?
Can you see the constellation Southern Cross from south of the
equator? How far is the magnetic north pole from the North Pole?

did you ☆   ❑   That no matter where you are in the northern latitudes, the
know?   direction north is always in the direction of the North Star.
    ❑   That the sun is our nearest star, but a spaceship traveling
25,000 miles (40,000 kilometers) an hour would still take about
five months to reach it. It would take about 115,000 years to
reach the next nearest star at the same speed.

Mount the camera on a tripod.

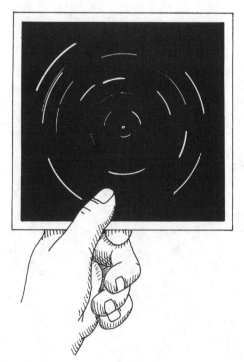

The North Star should be in the center of your photograph.

11
What is your horizon?

materials ☆   ❑ Lid from jar
              ❑ Basketball

procedure ☆   1. Place the lid right side up on top of the basketball. The ball
represents the earth. Imagine that you are very small and
standing on top of the ball at the exact center of the lid.

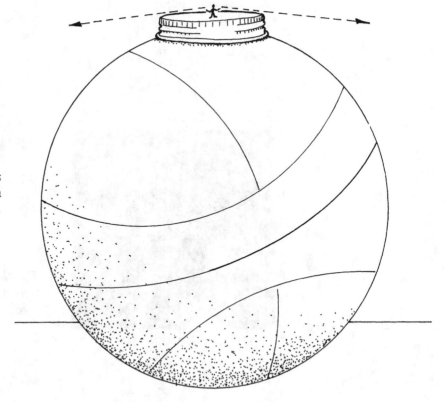

*Your horizon is
where the earth
meets the sky.*

results ☆ Everything in the sky above the lid would be visible to you. But you could not see anything over the edge of the lid. The edge of the lid forming a circle would be your *horizon*. No matter where we are, each one of us has a horizon. The horizon is the lowest point of the sky you can see. Your horizon is always a complete circle around you.

further ☆ Is there anywhere on earth where you can see the whole night sky?
studies Could you see it from along the equator? Can you see the North Star from the equator? Why does the moon look larger at the horizon than it does when it is higher in the sky?

did you ☆ ❏ That if you were in a small boat at sea with your eyes about 4
know? feet (1.2 meters) above the water, your horizon would be about 2½ miles (4 kilometers) away.
❏ That if you were in an airplane flying at about 5,000 feet (1,525 meters), you could see almost 100 miles (160 kilometers) to your horizon.

12
What is your latitude?

materials ☆
- ❏ Clear night
- ❏ Friend to help
- ❏ Large sheet of paper
- ❏ Pencil
- ❏ Protractor

procedure ☆
1. Locate the North Star and then stand facing that direction. Hold both arms straight out in front of you. Keep one arm level and point at the horizon. Hold your shoulders level and move your other arm up until your finger points at the North Star. Ask your friend to hold the paper up next to you and make three pencil marks on the paper—one even with your shoulders and one each at the ends of the fingers you are pointing.
2. Draw two lines from the dot representing your shoulder to the dots representing your pointing fingers. Measure the angle between the two lines with the protractor.

results ☆
The angle you measured is the approximate *latitude* of your location. Latitudes are imaginary lines that run around the earth parallel to the equator. Latitude is measured in *degrees*. Any point on the equator has a latitude of zero degrees. The North Pole has a latitude of 90 degrees north. The South Pole has a latitude of 90 degrees south. The distance between each degree is about 69 statute (land) miles (110 kilometers) or 60 nautical (sea or air) miles. The distances vary because the earth is not a perfect sphere.

further studies ☆
To a pilot, *altitude* means how high the plane is flying above the ground or above sea level, normally measured in feet. To an astronomer or navigator on the ground, altitude means how high something is above the horizon, measured in degrees. You can measure the approximate altitude of a star using the same method of finding your latitude, but only the altitude of the North Star

POLARIS

Use your arms to form the angle of the North Star.

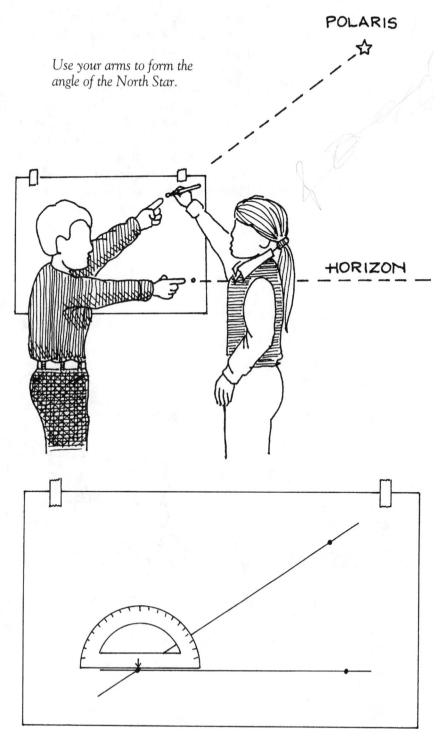

HORIZON

Mark the angle on the paper and measure it to find your latitude.

gives you your latitude. Why is this true? Look at a map or globe and find the latitudes of other cities. Can you find cities in other countries that are on your latitude?

did you ☆ know?

❑ That each degree of latitude is divided into 60 minutes, and each minute is divided into 60 seconds? Therefore, 1 minute of latitude equals about 1 nautical mile (1.8 kilometers).

❑ That early sailors would extend their arms, tuck their thumbs out of the way, and use their fingers to measure the altitude of a star and to measure time. Four fingers above the horizon equals about 15 degrees, or about 1 hour in time.

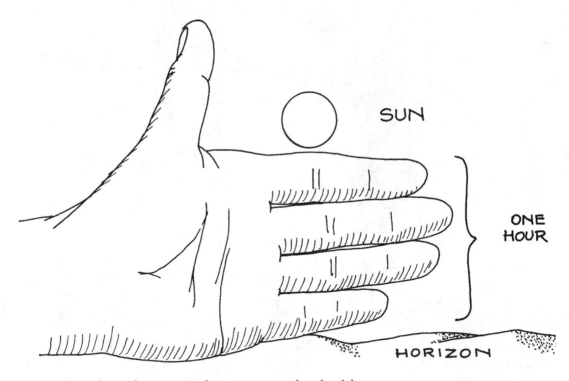

SUN

ONE HOUR

HORIZON

Your hand can be used to measure the approximate altitude of the sun or a star.

13
What is your meridian?

materials ☆
- ❏ Magnetic compass
- ❏ Sunny day
- ❏ Two straight sticks about 12 inches (30.48 cm) long
- ❏ Hammer

procedure ☆

1. Use the magnetic compass to mark a line in the dirt running north and south. A few minutes before noon, have an adult help you drive the two sticks straight into the ground, 3 or 4 inches (7.6 or 10 cm) apart, on this line.

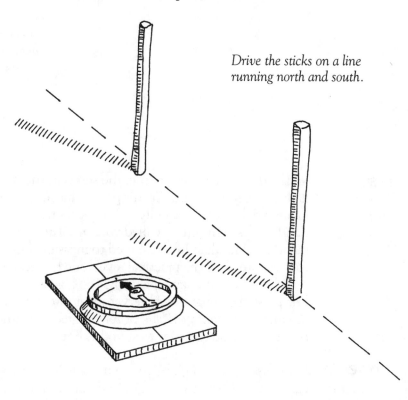

Drive the sticks on a line running north and south.

2. Watch the shadows of both sticks until the shadows are in line.

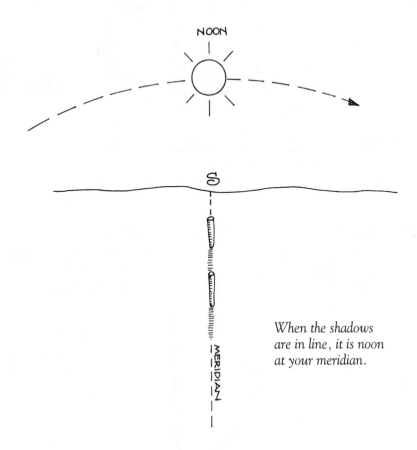

When the shadows are in line, it is noon at your meridian.

results ☆ When the shadows are in line, the sun is in the highest point in its daily arc across the sky. At this precise instant, the sun is crossing the imaginary line of a great circle that passes through the North and South Poles. This line is called your *meridian*. It is noon all along the meridian. Meridian lines are used to measure longitude (or distances east and west). To be practical, everyone had to start counting meridians from the same place. In 1884, geographers decided that a line passing through the observatory at Greenwich, England, would be called the *prime meridian*, or zero degrees longitude. Distances on a map are measured east or west of this line.

further ☆ studies Look at a map or a globe to see if you can find your *longitude*. Is it east or west? What is the longitude of New York City or of

London, England? If it is 12 noon in London, what time is it in New Zealand? Where does one day end and another begin? What is the international date line?

❑ That the 180th meridian (the international date line) zigzags in several places so that a country won't have two different calendar dates on the same day.

❑ That longitude is measured in degrees, minutes, and seconds just like latitude. But, unlike latitude lines, longitude lines are not parallel. Because the lines come together at the poles, the only place a degree equals about 69 miles (110 kilometers) is at the equator.

Part 3
The young chemist

Chemical change is all around us. Iron rusts, and coals burning in a furnace turn into ash, water vapor, and gases. Even the food we eat is chemically changed inside our bodies to give us energy and to make flesh and bone.

In the Middle Ages, chemistry was the tool of alchemists who were mainly concerned with trying to turn inexpensive base metals such as iron and lead into gold. Today, chemistry is in the hands of trained people conducting exciting research and making amazing discoveries. Chemists are developing alloys, plastics, and other materials for everyday use as well as new materials to be used in space. Even our health has been greatly improved through the discovery of new drugs and medicines. Many forms of fuel and energy would not be available without chemistry. The following experiments are easy introductions into the fascinating world of chemistry.

14
What are acids and bases?

materials ☆
- ❑ Water
- ❑ Teakettle and pan
- ❑ Stove
- ❑ Safety goggles
- ❑ Knife and large spoon
- ❑ Red cabbage
- ❑ Pot holders
- ❑ Two paper towels or coffee filters
- ❑ Funnel
- ❑ Bottle with lid
- ❑ Bowl
- ❑ Cookie sheet
- ❑ Scissors
- ❑ Plastic sandwich bag
- ❑ Two medicine droppers
- ❑ Paper
- ❑ Vinegar
- ❑ Household ammonia

procedure ☆

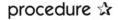

1. Adult assistance is needed throughout this experiment. Be sure to wear your safety goggles as well. To find out which things are acids or bases, you need an acid indicator. To make a liquid indicator, have an adult help you heat some water in the teakettle.

While the water is heating on the stove, chop up about one-fourth of the cabbage. Place the chopped cabbage in the pan, and then pour boiling water over the pieces of cabbage. Pour in just enough water to cover the cabbage. Use pot holders and be careful.

Boiling water can cause severe burns. Stir the cabbage pieces, then let them soak about 20 minutes.

Pour boiling water over the cabbage pieces.

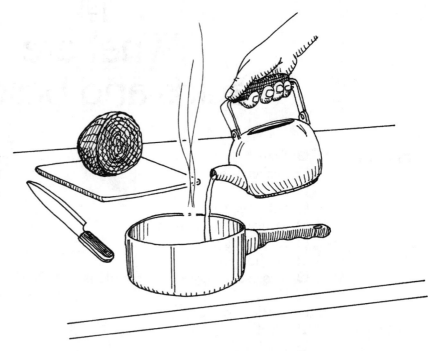

2. Make a filter by folding a paper towel twice, and then separate one of the corners to make a pocket. As an alternative, you can use a coffee filter. Place the filter inside the funnel, and then the funnel into the bottle. Ask an adult to help you pour the cabbage pieces and the purple-colored liquid through the funnel into the bottle. The filter will separate the cabbage pieces from the liquid. You can label the bottle as indicator and save it for future experiments. Allow the bottle to stand until the liquid cools to room temperature. The liquid should turn blue.

3. Pour about a cup of the indicator into the bowl. Soak a paper towel, or coffee filter, in the bowl. Then place the paper on a cookie sheet or similar surface to dry.

 4. After the paper has dried, cut it into strips about 1 inch wide and 4 inches long. The strips should be pale blue. They can be stored in the sandwich bag for future use.

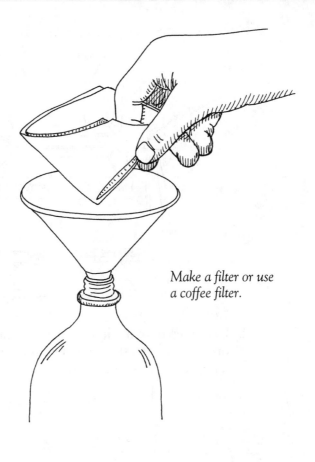

*Make a filter or use
a coffee filter.*

*Spread out the
paper and let it dry.*

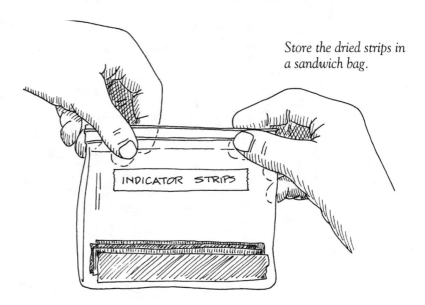

Store the dried strips in a sandwich bag.

INDICATOR STRIPS

5. Using separate medicine droppers, drop a few drops of vinegar on one end of a strip of paper and a couple drops of household ammonia on the other end.

Drop vinegar on one end and ammonia on the other.

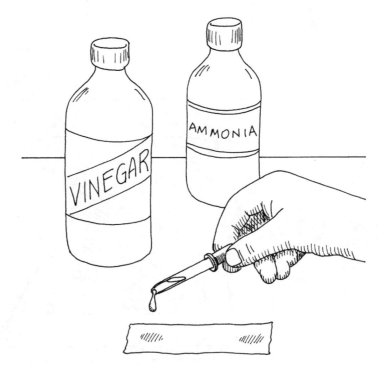

AMMONIA

VINEGAR

results ☆ An *acid* is a compound with a sharp, sour taste that neutralizes a *base*. A base is a chemical that tastes bitter and neutralizes an acid. The vinegar turned the paper pink and the ammonia turned it green. Cabbage juice can be used to test for the presence of acids or bases because it always causes the same color changes when reacting with acids or bases. Acids turn the test paper pink or red. Bases turn it green. This test shows that vinegar is acidic and that ammonia is basic.

further ☆ What colors would be produced on the test paper by pickle juice?
studies What colors would be produced by lemon juice, orange juice, or grapefruit juice? Test small solutions of baking soda and water, cream of tarter and water, or liquid soap to see if they are acids or bases.

did you ☆ ❑ That we drink an acid when we drink lemonade.
know? ❑ That the poison in a bee sting is an acid.
❑ That when two dangerous chemicals, sodium hydroxide and hydrochloric acid, are combined, they are neutralized and form sodium chloride (table salt).

15
What makes ice float?

materials ☆
- ❏ Tablespoon
- ❏ Salt
- ❏ Two drinking glasses
- ❏ Water
- ❏ Two ice cubes

procedure ☆   1. Pour a tablespoon of salt into one of the glasses and fill the glass with water. Stir the water until most of the salt dissolves.

Stir the salt solution.

2. Fill the other glass with plain tap water.

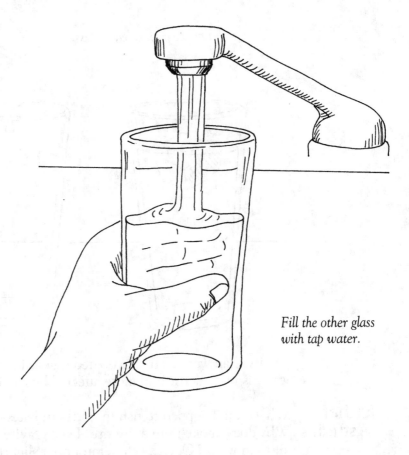

Fill the other glass with tap water.

3. Drop an ice cube into each glass and notice how high each cube floats in the water. Which ice cube floats highest in the water?

results ☆ The ice cube in the salt water should float higher than the one in plain water. Most things shrink when they get colder. For example, air *molecules* get smaller and become more dense when they get colder. Also, cold air sinks toward the earth. Because of *gravity*, heavier, more dense things are pulled down while forcing lighter, less dense things up.

When water freezes into ice, it expands and takes up more space than water. Ice floats because it is less dense and less affected by

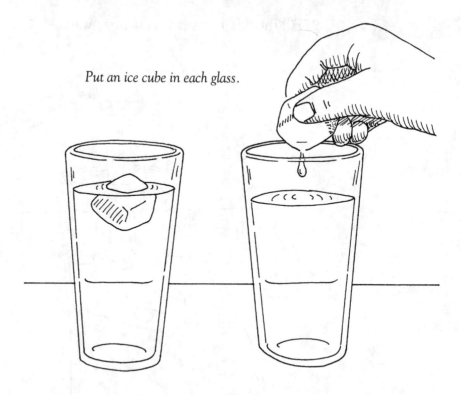

Put an ice cube in each glass.

gravity than water. The ice floated higher in salt water because salt water is more dense and more affected by gravity than plain water.

further ☆ studies

What would happen to fish in northern lakes if ice didn't float? Why does smoke from a fire rise? Does gravity pull harder on cold air than warm? Open a refrigerator door slightly and feel the air at the top and bottom of the door. Does air come out at the bottom of the door? Can you feel warm air being drawn in at the top of the door? Is gravity working here?

did you ☆ know?

❏ That if ice did not float, the seas would gradually turn to ice and no life could survive on earth.
❏ That metal pipes often burst when the water inside them freezes and the ice expands.
❏ That when water settles into cracks in a large boulder and freezes, the force from the expanding ice can split the boulder.

16
What is starch?

materials ☆
□ Paper towel or newspaper
□ Table
□ Knife
□ Foods to test (potato, apple, salt, flour, small piece of toasted white bread)
□ Salt
□ Flour
□ Water
□ Small jar
□ Iodine
□ Tablespoon
□ Medicine dropper

procedure ☆

1. Place the paper towel or newspaper on a table. Have an adult cut slices from the potato and apple and place them on the paper. Put the toasted bread on the paper and pour a small mound of salt and a mound of flour on the paper.

Place the objects to be tested on a paper towel.

2. Pour a little water in the jar, add an equal amount of iodine, and use a spoon to stir the solution.

Mix up an iodine solution.

3. Use the medicine dropper to put a drop of the iodine solution on the cut part of the potato and apple. Place a drop on the toast—where the white, inner part is exposed—add a drop on the mound of salt, and another drop on the mound of flour.

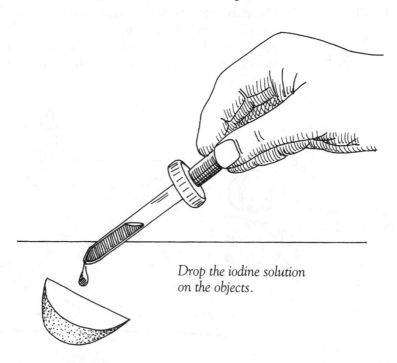

Drop the iodine solution on the objects.

results ☆ The foods that contain starch turned dark blue or purple. Foods without starch were only stained by the solution. The white center of the toast turned bluish purple, indicating starch. The toasted part should not change color. The heat from the toaster changed the starch in the crust into *dextrin*. Because dextrin and starch are both *carbohydrates*, the chemical makeup of dextrin is much like starch. Dextrin is easier to digest in our bodies. Dextrin forms during digestion by the action of saliva and other body fluids on starch. You might have noticed that only the foods that come from plants contain starch. Throw the tested foods away when you have finished.

further ☆ Use the iodine solution to test for starch in strips of notebook
studies paper, newspaper, and other types of paper. Did some of the drops turn bluish black or black? When some papers are made, a film of a starch solution is put on it to give the paper a smooth surface and to hold the fibers together.

did you ☆ ❑ That starch was used in ancient times. As early as 184 B.C.,
know? Marcus Porcius Cato the Elder, a prominent figure in Rome, described the preparation of starch from cereal grains.

Marcus Porcius Cato the Elder

❑ That the manufacture of starch in the United States began in the early 1800s.
❑ That starch is made only in those plants that contain *chlorophyll*.

17
What is carbon?

materials ☆ ❏ Candle mounted on lid
              ❏ Match
              ❏ Sugar
              ❏ Metal pan
              ❏ Old metal spoon
              ❏ Pot holder

procedure ☆ 1. Ask an adult for permission to light the candle. Notice how the flame burns.

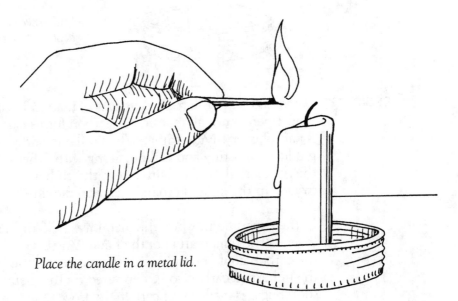

Place the candle in a metal lid.

2. Hold the metal pan in the flame for a few seconds and then set it aside.
3. Pour a small amount of sugar in the spoon. Spread it out with your finger so that it makes a thin layer. Using a pot holder,

hold the spoon over the candle and heat the sugar until it stops smoking. Remove the spoon from the flame and set the spoon on a surface that will not melt or scorch.

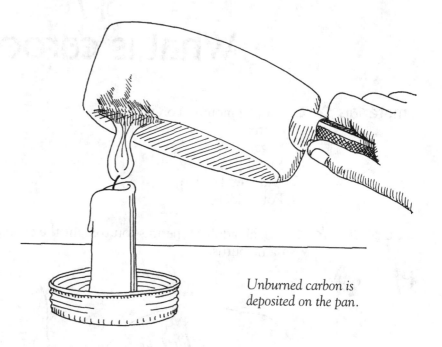

Unburned carbon is deposited on the pan.

results ☆ *Carbon* is one of the basic elements of matter. It makes up less than 1 percent of all matter, but carbon forms part of all foods and is part of every living thing. When a flame burns, the flame produces moisture and carbon, along with other substances. When the flame is allowed to burn freely, the carbon mixes with the oxygen in the air and produces carbon dioxide.

In the experiment, when the metal was held in the flame, it lowered the temperature of the flame. At this cooler temperature, the carbon could not mix with the oxygen in the air. This causes the unburned carbon to be deposited on the metal in the form of soot. Sugar is made up of carbon, hydrogen, and oxygen. When you heat the sugar, it first turns into a clear liquid. Then it turns brown and begins to bubble. Puffs of smoke come up from the liquid, which then turns black. The heat from the flame changes the hydrogen and oxygen in the sugar into a vapor. As the vapor bubbles away into the air, carbon remains on the spoon in the form of a charred, lumpy mass.

further ☆ studies What other things can you think of that contain carbon? Can graphite be used as a lubricant? Is coal a form of carbon? When carbon combines with hydrogen, it forms compounds called *hydrocarbons*. Does oil or gasoline contain hydrocarbons?

did you ☆ know?
❑ That a radioactive isotope of carbon (carbon-14) is used as a means of dating archaeological specimens and fossils.
❑ That pure carbon occurs in nature in the form of diamonds and black graphite.
❑ That carbon was discovered in ancient times.

18
What is
carbon dioxide?

materials ☆   ❏ Vinegar
                 ❏ Jar
                 ❏ Teaspoon
                 ❏ Baking soda

procedure ☆   1. Pour enough vinegar into the jar to cover the bottom about
                   ¼ inch (.635 cm).
                2. Add a few teaspoons of baking soda to the vinegar.

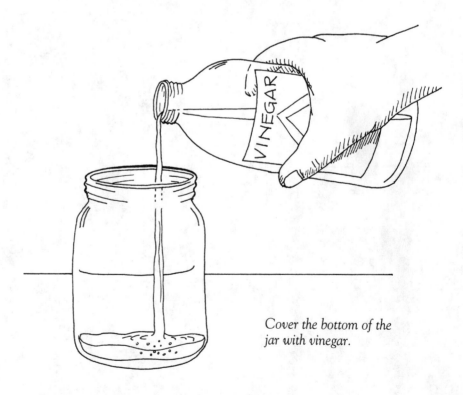

*Cover the bottom of the
jar with vinegar.*

Baking soda and vinegar produces carbon dioxide gas.

results ☆ The mixture quickly begins to fizz and bubble. It is generating carbon dioxide gas, and, as the gas escapes, it makes the mixture bubble. *Carbon dioxide* is a colorless, odorless, incombustible gas. It is about one and a half times heavier than air.

Carbon dioxide is produced in an important exchange between animals and plants. All animals, including us, breath oxygen in and breath out carbon dioxide. The plants absorb this carbon dioxide and use it for *photosynthesis*. The plants, in turn, give off oxygen. This exchange keeps a fairly stable supply of oxygen and carbon dioxide in the air. Both plants and animals need oxygen for respiration. In air that contains large amounts of carbon dioxide, people and animals quickly suffocate. The gas itself is not poisonous; carbon dioxide simply cuts off the supply of oxygen to the bloodstream.

further ☆
studies   Because carbon dioxide is heavier than air, could pockets of this gas accumulate in mine shafts? Would this condition be dangerous? If carbon dioxide displaces oxygen, will it put out a candle? Could carbon dioxide be used in fire extinguishers?

did you ☆
know?   ❏ That carbon dioxide can be frozen. It is called *dry ice*. When dry ice melts, it does not form a liquid, but turns directly into a gas.
    ❏ That carbon dioxide is used to give the sparkle and biting taste to bubbly drinks such as colas. That is why they are called *carbonated beverages*.

19
What is water?

materials ☆
- ❏ Safety goggles
- ❏ Scissors
- ❏ Two flexible copper wires about 18 inches (45.72 cm) long
- ❏ 9-volt battery
- ❏ Tape
- ❏ Two small paper clips
- ❏ Two pencil leads from mechanical pencil or two pencils sharpened on both ends
- ❏ Clear drinking glass or jar
- ❏ Tap water

procedure ☆

1. Wear your safety goggles throughout this experiment. Have an adult use the scissors to carefully trim about 1 inch (2.54 cm) of the insulation from each end of the wires.
2. Connect a wire to each terminal on the battery. Twist the bare ends around the terminals to make them tight. Use tape to hold the connections in place.
3. Connect the remaining bare ends to each of the paper clips (one wire, one paper clip). Clamp a paper clip to each of the pencil leads.
4. Fill the glass nearly to the top with water. Position each paper clip on the rim of the glass so that the leads extend down into the water.

results ☆ Water is a compound of *hydrogen* and *oxygen*. In the experiment, bubbles began forming on the pencil leads. One lead has about twice as many bubbles as the other. Also, one lead is collecting oxygen bubbles while the other is creating hydrogen bubbles. An electrical current flows from the battery, down through the pencil lead, through the water, to the other pencil lead, and back to the battery.

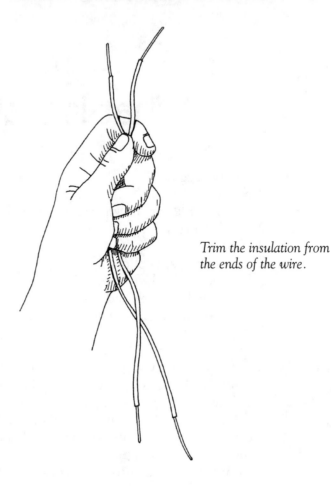

Trim the insulation from the ends of the wire.

Water (and everything else) is made up of tiny particles called *atoms*. These atoms cling together and form molecules. Each water molecule is made up of one oxygen atom and two hydrogen atoms. When the electrical current flows from the battery, the water molecules separate into atoms of oxygen and hydrogen. Water has twice as many hydrogen atoms as oxygen atoms. Therefore, twice as many hydrogen bubbles form as do oxygen bubbles.

further ☆ studies All air contains some water vapor, but the amount varies greatly. The amount of water vapor in the air is called *humidity*. Warm air can hold more moisture than cold air. Do you feel more comfortable on warm, humid days than on dry days? Are our bodies water-cooled? How much of your body is water? How many gallons of water per person do you think your family uses each day?

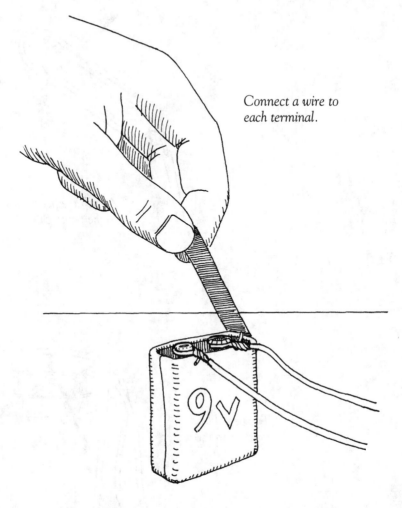

Connect a wire to each terminal.

did you ☆ know?

- ❑ That about 70 percent of the earth is covered with water.
- ❑ That the Pacific Ocean covers nearly half the earth.
- ❑ That no new water is ever made. The water cycle on earth uses the water over and over again. Water evaporates from forests, lakes, and oceans, turns into clouds, falls as rain and snow, flows down rivers and trickles through the soil, then returns to the forests, lakes, and oceans. The rain that falls today has fallen millions of times before.

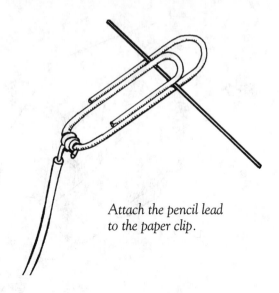

*Attach the pencil lead
to the paper clip.*

*The pencil leads
must be in the water.*

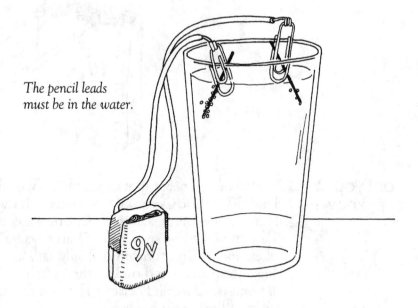

Part 4
The young meteorologist

Meteorology is the exciting study of the weather and the atmosphere. Meteorologists try to learn as much about the atmosphere as they can. They use *thermometers* to measure temperature, *anemometers* to measure wind speed, *barometers* to measure atmospheric pressure, and *hygrometers* to measure the moisture content of the air. Pilots, sea captains, farmers, and highway departments are just a few of the people concerned with weather conditions and the science of meteorology.

Even the space shuttle has had its launching and landings delayed by weather. Large gas and electric companies use weather forecasts to determine how much energy they must have available to supply the public needs. What we do, how we live, and even where we live is, in some way, dependent on the weather conditions and the science of meteorology.

20
What are clouds?

materials ☆
❑ Glass jug with small mouth
❑ Match or candle

procedure ☆

1. Turn the jug upside down. Ask an adult for permission to light a match or candle. Carefully hold the jug opening over the flame of a match or candle for only a few seconds. Be sure to put out the match before it burns your fingers or move the candle before the jug becomes too hot to hold.

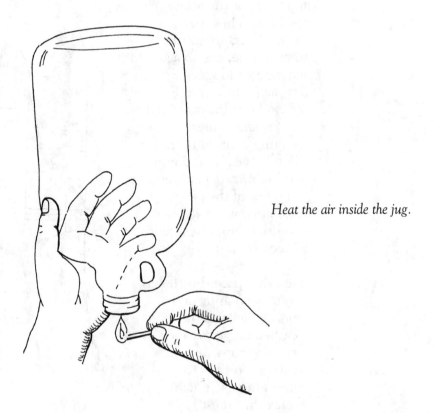

Heat the air inside the jug.

2. Remove the flame, take a deep breath, and quickly place your mouth over the opening, making a tight seal.

Make a tight seal over the opening of the jug.

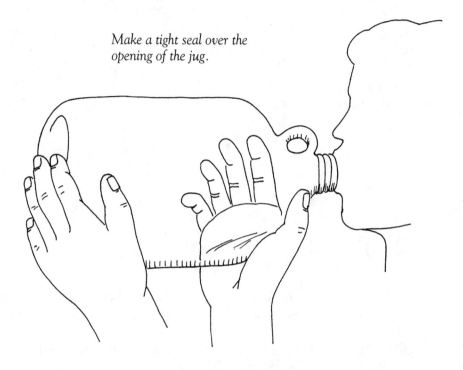

3. Blow hard into the jug; be careful not to breath in. You want to compress the air inside as much as possible. Then abruptly remove your mouth and release the pressure.

results ☆ Clouds form when warm air rises in the sky and then cools down enough for some of the water vapor in the air to condense into tiny drops of water. In the experiment, when you release the pressure, a cloud forms. As you compress the air in the jug, you also add moisture from your breath. When you suddenly release the pressure, the air in the jug expands and cools. The cooler air can't hold as much moisture as the warm air. Therefore, some of the moisture condenses into tiny droplets and forms a cloud.

further ☆ studies Notice the clouds in your area. Why are some clouds shaped differently than others? What is the thin layer of clouds called that forms when a large mass of air rises slowly? What is the name of

Blow hard, and then quickly remove your mouth. A cloud forms.

the thick, towering clouds that form when small masses of warm air rise quickly? Do *cumulonimbus* clouds usually bring rain?

did you ☆ know?

❑ That the tallest cloud, the giant cumulonimbus, can reach a height of 50,000 feet.

❑ That fog is really a low cloud that forms when the air at or just above the earth's surface cools.

❑ That early sailors used clouds to find land, because clouds often form above islands.

21
What are rain, snow, and hail?

materials ☆ ❏ Water
❏ Saucepan
❏ Stove
❏ Metal funnel
❏ Refrigerator
❏ Ice cubes
❏ Plastic sandwich bag
❏ Four paper clips
❏ Fruit jar

procedure ☆ 1. Have an adult heat some water to almost a boil. While the water is heating, place the funnel in a freezer, and place two or three ice cubes inside the sandwich bag.

Bring the water to nearly a boil.

2. Open the four paper clips and place them equal distances around the rim of the jar. The paper clips keep the funnel from forming a seal.

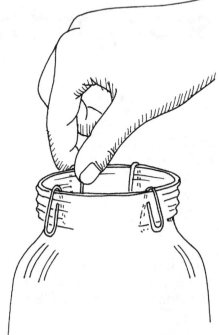

Place the paper clips around the rim of the jar.

3. Have an adult fill the jar about half full of steaming water. Fit the bag of ice into the mouth of the funnel and place the funnel into the opening of the jar.

results ☆ Clouds develop when warm, moist air rises and begins to cool. If enough moisture is present, and if the air continues to cool, tiny water droplets combine and form larger raindrops. When the droplets become heavy enough, they fall to the earth as rain. Rain can also form when larger ice crystals melt.

In the experiment, the hot water supplies the moist air and the ice in the funnel provides the cooling. Moisture forms on the side of the funnel until it grows into drops that fall back into the jar as homemade rain. Snow crystals form when water freezes onto tiny ice particles in a cloud. As they become larger and start to fall,

Place the funnel and the ice bag in the jar to make rain.

they attach to other crystals and become snowflakes and fall to the earth. Sometimes the flakes fall through warmer air, melt, and turn into freezing rain or rain.

Hail forms only in cumulonimbus clouds. Hail develops when ice crystals are tossed up and down many times inside the cloud. As the ice crystals bounce up and down, water freezes on the crystals in layers. The layers build up, like the skins of an onion, until the ice becomes heavy enough to fall as hail.

further ☆ studies Listen to a weather report. Is your state above or below its average rainfall? Does rain cause erosion? Are some countries having floods while others are experiencing droughts?

did you ☆ know? ❑ That in the rain forests of South America, it rains almost every day, for an annual rainfall from 80 to 150 inches (2.032 to 3.81 meters).

❑ That small fish and frogs have fallen along with the rain in some rainstorms.
❑ That raindrops are not tear-shaped, as often pictured, but are half round and flat on the bottom.

The young meteorologist

22
What is the Coriolis force?

materials ☆
- ❏ Globe of the earth
- ❏ Piece of chalk

procedure ☆
1. Place one hand on top of the globe and slowly turn it counterclockwise, looking down at the North Pole. The earth spins in this direction.
2. As you turn the globe, draw a chalk line down from the North Pole to the equator. Next, draw a line up from the South Pole to the equator.

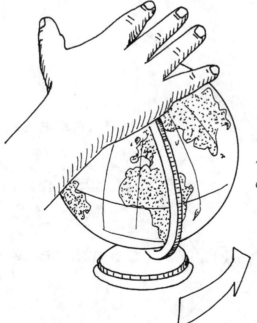

Turn the globe counterclockwise.

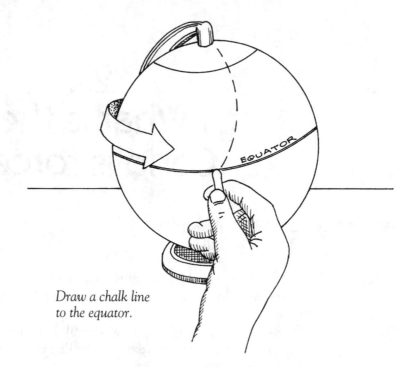

*Draw a chalk line
to the equator.*

3. Stop the globe and notice the curve in each chalk line.

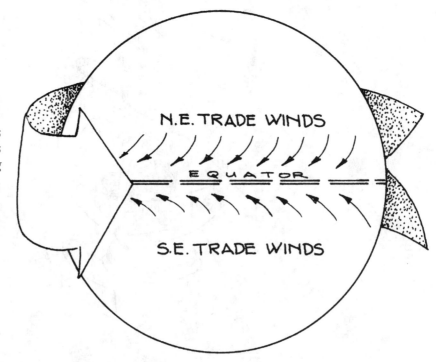

*The Coriolis
force causes winds
to curve along
the equator.*

N.E. TRADE WINDS

EQUATOR

S.E. TRADE WINDS

results ☆ The warm air near the equator is lighter than the cooler air near the poles. This condition creates a permanent low-pressure area, called the *equatorial low*, around the earth near the equator. The cooler air at the poles sinks to the earth to form areas of *polar highs*. This heavier air moves toward the equator and forces the warmer air upward into the upper atmosphere. This warm air moves toward the poles, cools, and sinks back to the earth.

Air currents move from the poles to the equator and back to the poles in a continuous cycle. However, these currents do not travel directly north or south. The currents are curved along the equator by an effect called the *Coriolis force*. The Coriolis force is the bending of the winds caused by the earth spinning on its axis. This force causes the air currents to curve to the right when moving down from the North Pole and curve to the left when coming up from the South pole. The force was named after French mathematician Gaspard G. Coriolis, who first analyzed the effect.

In the experiment, turning the globe represents the earth spinning on its *axis*. The curved chalk lines represent the path of air currents from the poles caused by the Coriolis force.

further studies ☆ What are the *trade winds*? Does much wind normally blow in equatorial regions? What are *equatorial calms*? Does air move constantly up along the equator?

did you know? ☆ ❏ That early sailors used trade winds to guide them across oceans.
❏ That Columbus might never have discovered America without the trade winds.

23
What are highs, lows, and fronts?

materials ☆   ❑ Weather map from a newspaper

procedure ☆   1. Look at the weather map and notice a pattern of wavy lines called *isobars*. Look for lines that make a large circle. Look for small circles.
                2. Examine the map further and find the letters "H" and "L." Look for keys on the edge of the map that display symbols representing the various weather conditions. Do you see any showers, thunderstorms, or snow storms?

Examine the weather map from your newspaper.

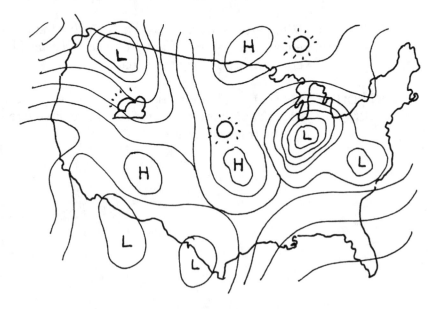

RAIN   STORMS   SNOW   ICE   SUNNY   P.CLOUDY   CLOUDY

results ☆ The isobars connect places that have the same air pressures. An area of high pressure can be thought of as a mountain of air. High-pressure air is heavier and rises above the surrounding air mass. Winds in a high-pressure area spiral outward and downward, causing clouds to evaporate and usually bringing fair weather. The farther apart the lines are, the lighter the winds.

When the lines are close together, the winds are strong, and the pressure is normally low. An area of low pressure can be thought of as a valley. The air is lighter than the surrounding air mass and causes winds to spiral inward, making the air in the center of the low rise. The rising air cools and often condenses into fog, clouds, or rain. Low pressure areas usually bring wet, stormy weather.

A *front* is the boundary between two different air masses. A cold front occurs when a mass of cold air pushes its way underneath a warmer mass of air. This pushes the warm air upward and, as the front moves, the cold air replaces the warm air. Rising warm air causes a narrow line of clouds to form along the front. Often, the result is violent rainstorms.

A cold front

A warm front forms when a mass of warm air overtakes and rides up over the top of a mass of cold air. The rising warm air causes clouds and sometimes violent thunderstorms to form in a wide area of the front.

WARM
FRONT

WARM AIR

COLD AIR

A warm front

**further ☆
studies**
If you know which way a front is moving, can you predict the weather ahead of the front? Is the eye of a *hurricane* the center of a low-pressure area? Does temperature affect the weather more than anything else?

**did you ☆
know?**
❑ That winds in low-pressure areas rotate counterclockwise in the northern hemisphere and clockwise in the southern hemisphere. The winds in highs blow clockwise in the northern hemisphere and counterclockwise in the southern hemisphere.

❑ That *tornadoes* usually form along a cold front. A current of cold air juts ahead of the front and rises above warm, moist air. The cold air aloft mixes with the warm air to form a whirling funnel with winds up to 300 miles (482.7 kilometers) an hour.

24
What is the dew point?

materials ☆
- ❏ Paper towel
- ❏ Ice cubes
- ❏ Tablespoon
- ❏ Bowl
- ❏ Shiny metal can
- ❏ Cool water
- ❏ Thermometer

procedure ☆ 1. The ice cubes should be broken into smaller pieces. Lay the paper towel across one hand, place an ice cube on the towel, and then hit the ice cube sharply with the back of the spoon. The ice should shatter into smaller pieces. Place the crushed ice in the bowl. Fill the bowl about half full of crushed ice.

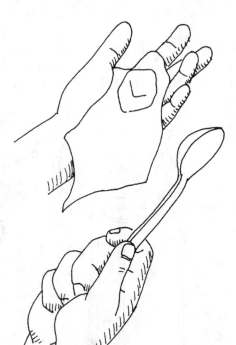

Use the back of a spoon to break the ice cubes.

2. Make sure the outside of the can is dry. Next, fill the can about one-fourth full of cool water. Place the thermometer in the can.

Place the thermometer in the can.

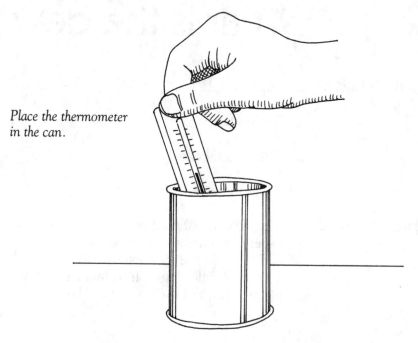

3. Slowly add the crushed ice to the water and stir until a thin layer of moisture forms on the outside of the can. Read the thermometer the instant the moisture forms.

Add ice and watch the thermometer.

results ☆ The *dew point* is the temperature at which water vapor in the air starts to condense into liquid. As air cools at night, the air gets to the temperature where it cannot hold any more water vapor. The vapor condenses into dew. When you add ice to the can, the can cools the air enough so that dew forms on the side of the can. The temperature at the instant the dew forms is the dew point. Meteorologists find the dew point by cooling the air until the water vapor begins to condense. The dew point temperature is not a fixed temperature but changes from day to day. It depends on the amount of moisture in the air.

further ☆ Can you add salt to the ice and produce frost? Does the weather
studies report in your newspaper show the dew point? Does the amount of moisture in the air affect how comfortable we feel?

did you ☆ ❏ That in areas where homes use evaporative coolers to cool the
know? house, the coolers become ineffective when the dew point temperature rises above 55 degrees F (13 degrees C).
❏ That farmers in the Canary Islands collect dew to water their crops.

25
What is a rainbow?

materials ☆ ❑ Morning or afternoon sunlight
❑ Garden hose with a spray nozzle

procedure ☆ 1. Turn your back to the sun and adjust the spray from the hose to
a fine mist. Spray the mist up in the air in front of you.

*Spray the mist up into
the air.*

results ☆ *Rainbows* are formed by the sun's rays when the rays are bent as they strike the drops of water. As a ray from the sun passes into a drop of rain, the water acts like a tiny *prism*. The ray is bent, or refracted, as it enters the drop and is separated into different colors.

When the ray strikes the inside surface of the drop, it is turned back, or reflected. As the ray leaves the drop, it is bent again. You can only see the colors that bend in your direction, which is why you can only see a rainbow with the sun behind you. The height of a rainbow depends on how high the sun is. The higher the sun, the lower the rainbow. If the sun is higher than 40 degrees, you won't see a rainbow.

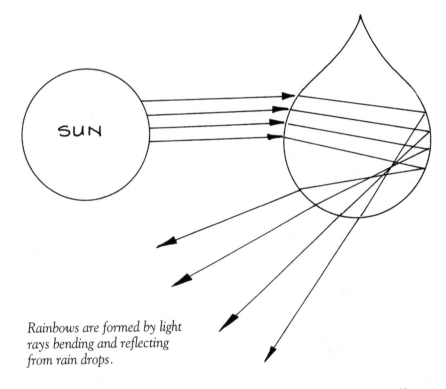

Rainbows are formed by light rays bending and reflecting from rain drops.

Rainbows give off seven colors: violet, indigo, blue, green, yellow, orange, and red. Each color is formed by rays that reach the eye at a certain angle, and the angle for that particular color never changes. When you spray the water in front of you, an arch of brilliant color appears in the mist.

further ☆ Can you see a rainbow around noon? Set a glass of water in a
studies sunny window. Will the water bend and separate the light rays like
a prism? Could you see a rainbow on a sunny day at Niagara Falls?

did you ☆ ❑ That if the sun was near the horizon, and you were in an
know? airplane, you might see the whole arc of a rainbow.
❑ That rainbows normally last only a few minutes.
❑ That sometimes the light of the moon forms a rainbow. It is
difficult to see because of the faintness of the light.

Part 5
The young biologist

Biology is the study of living things. It describes the origin, physical characteristics, habits, and life processes of plants and animals. Biology is one of the oldest sciences. Even our earliest ancestors were interested in the wonders of plants and animals. One of the great wonders of the universe is how living things take in food, grow, and reproduce their own kind. As equipment and instruments become more advanced, scientists can probe deeper into the curious phenomenon called life.

The young biologist

26
What is photosynthesis?

materials ☆
- ❑ Potted plant (bean plants work well)
- ❑ Two 1-inch (2.54 cm) paper squares
- ❑ Paper clip

procedure ☆
1. Near the top of the plant, place one paper on top of a leaf and the other on the bottom of the same leaf. Fasten the papers in place with the paper clip.
2. Place the plant in a sunny location for a few days.
3. Remove the paper clip and the pieces of paper. Examine the leaf.

results ☆ Green plants must have water, minerals, and chlorophyll to make food. To make chlorophyll, plants must have light. The green leaves change light energy into chemical energy and the chemical energy is used to make food. The process is called photosynthesis. The term *photosynthesis* means "putting together by light." When you remove the papers, you noticed the area they covered is a lighter color. Because no light got through the paper, the area was unable to produce chlorophyll.

Chlorophyll, which mean "light-green leaf," forms tiny green specks grouped against the inside walls of the cells in the leaf. They give the leaf its green color. Photosynthesis is the process a plant uses to manufacture food from sunlight and chlorophyll. The process produces sugar and starch (the food) from carbon dioxide and water. Your experiment shows that without sunlight and chlorophyll, photosynthesis can't take place.

further studies ☆ Do mushrooms use photosynthesis to make food? Do they live off food made by green-leaf plants? Leave a plant near a window for a few days. Does the plant bend toward the sunlight? Turn the plant around. Does the plant bend back?

did you ☆
know?

❏ That some parts of many familiar plants we eat every day contain poisons.

❏ That Daniel Boone (1734–1820), the most famous pioneer of colonial times, after all of his adventures, died at the age of 86 from eating too many sweet potatoes.

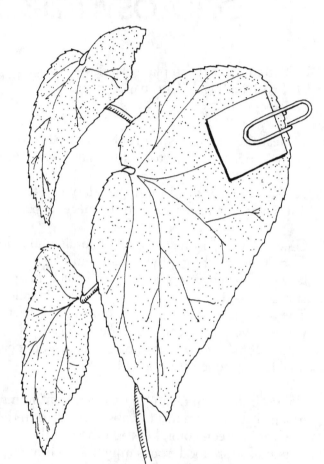

Fasten the papers in place with a paper clip.

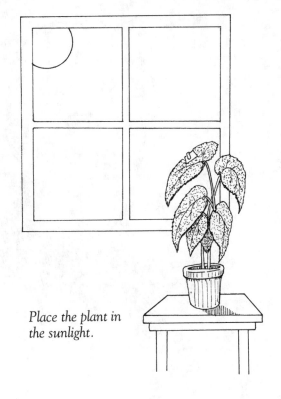

Place the plant in the sunlight.

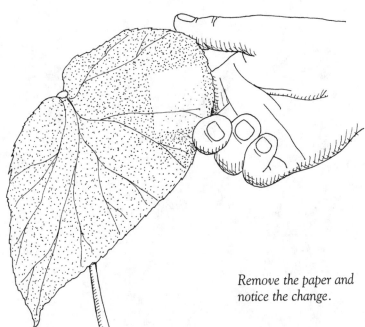

Remove the paper and notice the change.

Daniel Boone

27
What do rings in a tree show?

materials ☆ ❑ The trunk of a tree that has been cut down or a tree stump

procedure ☆ 1. Look closely at the rings in the trunk. You should see dark rings separated by lighter bands. Notice the width of some of the bands.

Examine the rings in the trunk.

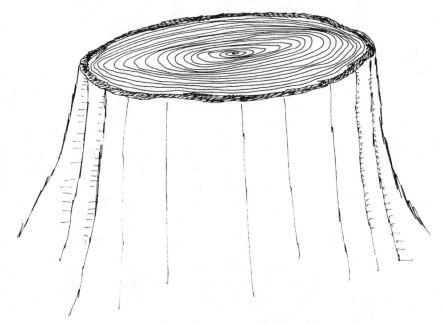

2. Begin at the center and count a light band and a dark ring as one year.

results ☆ Just under the bark of the tree is a layer of growing tissue called *cambium*. Cambium is made up of living cells that add a new ring of wood to the trunk each year. This way the trunk, roots, and

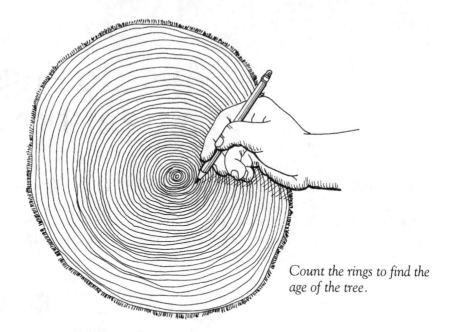

Count the rings to find the age of the tree.

branches grow thicker. When you count the rings, start at the center ring, which was the tree's first year of growth. The dark ring shows the growth in summer and the light band shows the growth in spring.

As you count outward from the center, you might discover that some rings are closer together than others. Where the rings are close together, it shows when the tree grew more slowly as it was competing with other plants and trees for sunlight, minerals, and water. If no other trees were close by while the tree was growing, the bands should be wider, showing a faster rate of growth.

Weather also affects the growth of trees. During dry years, the bands are narrow, showing that the tree grew more slowly. If the tree was able to reach its full size, the growth slows again and the bands become narrower.

The wood inside the trunk is filled with small pipe-like cells. These cells provide connections through which sap from the roots can rise. The layers of living cells (the *phloem*) just inside the bark carry food from the leaves to all parts of the tree. The trunk acts like a two-lane road. Sap moves up inside the trunk through tiny pipes in the wood. Food travels down outside the wood just under the bark.

further ☆ ❏ Rings in the tree can tell you the tree's life story. Can you find
studies any signs in the trunk where the tree was damaged by insects or
decay? How long did your tree live? Will a tree die if the bark is
cut through to the wood all the way around the trunk? Is the
tree's food supply cut off?

did you ☆ ❏ Redwood trees are the tallest plants on earth. They can grow
know? more than 300 feet (91.5 meters) high, or about as high as a 30-
story building.
❏ That before a law was passed that protected sequoia trees, a
certain giant sequoia was cut down. By counting the rings, it
was found that the tree dated back to 1305 B.C. The tree was
more than a thousand years old at the time of the birth of
Christ.
❏ That trees never stop growing as long as they live.

28
What are lungs for?

materials ☆
- ❏ Small tube about 8 inches (20.32 cm) long
- ❏ Cork stopper with hole
- ❏ Modeling clay or melted candle wax
- ❏ Two liter plastic soft drink bottle
- ❏ Balloon
- ❏ Utility knife
- ❏ String
- ❏ Large balloon to fit over bottom of bottle
- ❏ Tape

procedure ☆

1. Insert the tube through the hole in the cork. If the tube doesn't fit tight, seal it with modeling clay or melted candle wax. Slide the balloon over the end of the tube and tie it in place with the string. Now press the cork into the top of the bottle.
2. Have an adult carefully cut out the bottom of the bottle.
3. Tie a knot in the center of the bottom of the larger balloon to serve as a handle. Stretch the balloon over the opening in the bottom of the bottle, leaving the knot on the outside. Have someone help you wrap string around the bottle to hold the balloon in place. Use tape to seal the edges. Hold the knot and slowly push into the bottle, and then gradually pull back out.

results ☆
Human beings have two lungs. They rest on a strong, muscular *diaphragm* that separates the chest and stomach cavities. The lungs supply the body cells with oxygen. Every time we take a breath, fresh air containing oxygen enters the lungs. The oxygen then travels down tubes that divide into smaller tubes like upside down branches on a tree. The smaller tubes finally lead into tiny hollows called *air sacs*. The oxygen then seeps through the thin walls of the air sacs and is absorbed by the blood. The blood circulates through the body, giving up oxygen and absorbing carbon dioxide.

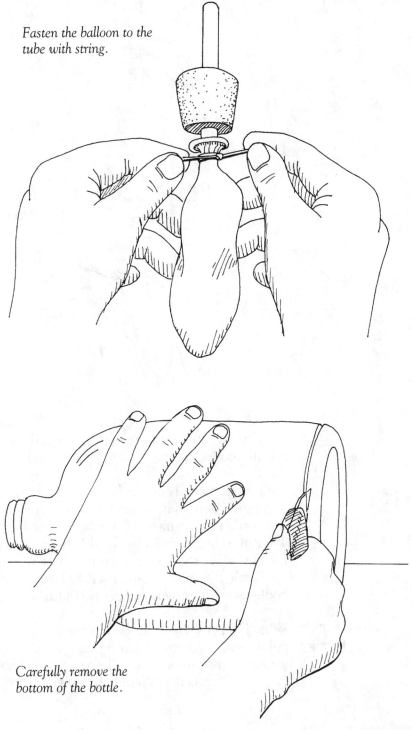

Fasten the balloon to the tube with string.

Carefully remove the bottom of the bottle.

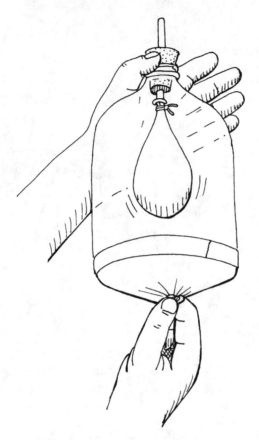

Pull on the knot to inflate the lung.

Blood then returns to the lungs to shed the carbon dioxide and to take in more oxygen.

For simplicity, only one balloon is used to represent the lungs in this experiment. The larger balloon stretched over the bottom of the bottle represents the diaphragm. The lungs have no muscles. They must be operated by the diaphragm. When you push in on the bottom of the bottle, then pull back out, the balloon inside the bottle fills with air and then deflates. This process is how our bodies take in oxygen and get rid of carbon dioxide.

**further ☆
studies** What happens when our bodies are deprived of oxygen? Is air pollution dangerous? What forms of air pollution can you find in your area? Is it important to know *cardiopulmonary resuscitation* (CPR)? What is the "Heimlich maneuver?"

❏ That if the walls of the tiny air sacs in the lungs could be spread out flat, they would cover more than 2,000 square feet (185.8 square meters). Doctors have estimated that a person's lungs contain more than 600 million air sacs.

❏ That the lungs are very elastic and stretch like balloons when filled with air.

❏ That a man's lungs weigh only about 3½ pounds. A woman's lungs weigh about 2¾ pounds. In proportion to their size, the lungs are the lightest organs in the human body.

29
What does
our heart do?

materials ☆
- ❑ Length of rubber tubing
- ❑ Two plastic funnels
- ❑ Watch with second hand
- ❑ Pencil and paper

procedure ☆   1. Connect the rubber tubing to the small ends of the funnel to make a simple *stethoscope*. Place the open end of one funnel over your heart and the other funnel over one ear.

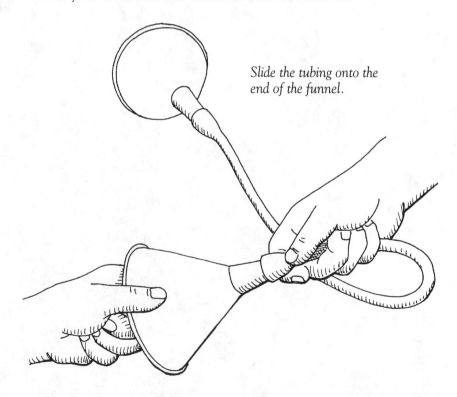

Slide the tubing onto the end of the funnel.

2. Count the number of heart beats you hear in one minute and write the number down. Exercise for several seconds, and then count the number of beats in one minute. Compare the numbers.

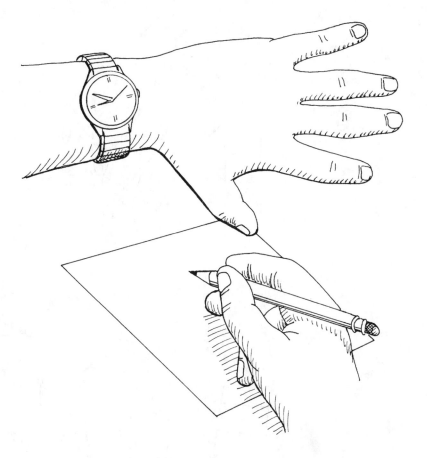

Record your heart rate.

3. Swing one arm in wide circles a couple of times. Let your arm hang down limp for a few seconds. Examine the top of that hand. Notice a few blue lines just under the skin. These are blood veins.

4. Press the tip of your finger down on one of the veins near your wrist. Push your finger along the vein toward the knuckles. The vein seems to disappear. Release your finger and the vein instantly fills back up.

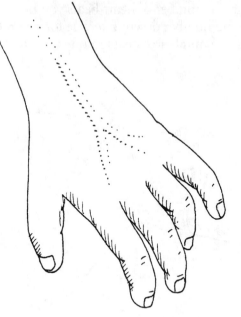

Find the blood veins on top of your hand.

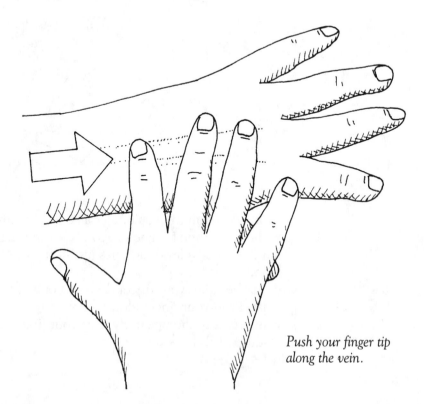

Push your finger tip along the vein.

results ☆ The walls of the heart are made up of a muscle that contracts, or beats, regularly and automatically. A normal human heart beats about 70 to 80 times a minute. The rate changes depending on the need for the blood to supply the body with oxygen and remove carbon dioxide. The oxygen combines with nutrients, or food, in the body cells to produce energy. When you exercise, your body needs more energy, so your heart beats faster.

In the experiment, when you move your finger down the vein from your wrist toward your knuckles, the vein empties of blood. The vein refills when you release the pressure. This simple experiment shows that the blood in your veins flows up the arm. The veins have valves that allow the blood to flow in one direction only: to the heart.

Blood circulates throughout your body through a system of tubes. The larger tubes, some as big as your thumb, are called *arteries*. Arteries carry blood away from the heart. The arteries become smaller and smaller as they reach into all areas of the body. The blood moves in spurts caused by the heart. The blood flows into a tiny mesh of tubes called *capillaries*. The capillaries is where the blood delivers nutrients to the body cells and picks up waste.

Next, the blood flows into veins like the one in the top of your hand. It is a steady flow without a pulse. The veins carry blood back through the lungs—in order to remove carbon dioxide and add oxygen—and then on to the heart. At the heart, the blood starts its trip all over again.

further ☆ Does your heart rate slow down when you are asleep? Does this
studies slower pace conserve energy? How are some animals able to hibernate? Animals that hibernate have hearts that scarcely beat. Do they breathe much slower? Where do they get their energy?

did you ☆ ❑ That the normal heart pumps about 5 quarts (4.73 liters) of
know? blood through the body in about 60 seconds.
❑ That the heart pumps blood through about 100,000 miles (160,900 kilometers) of blood vessels; 100,000 miles is about the same distance as five round trips between Sydney, Australia, and New York City.
❑ That the heart does enough work in 12 hours to lift more than 100,000 pounds 12 inches (30.48 cm) off the ground.

Part 6
The young physicist

Physics is a term that comes from a Greek word meaning nature. Physics is the science that explores the natural world around us. It tells us the how spiders can walk on water, how sound waves travel, what light is, and why a satellite stays in orbit. Prehistoric people probably wondered how they could skip a flat rock across a body of water or why stars twinkle. Physics is the study of the exciting natural world around us.

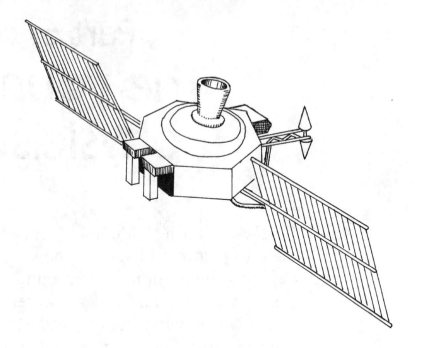

The young physicist

30
What is
surface tension?

materials ☆   ❑ Bowl of water
            ❑ Steel needle

procedure ☆   1. Allow the water to settle into a smooth surface. Make sure the needle is clean and dry.

Allow the water to calm.

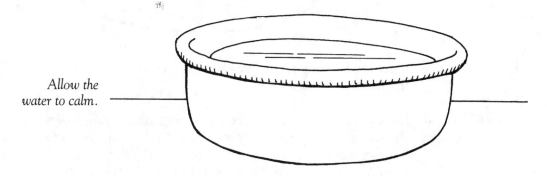

2. Hold the needle lightly between your thumb and finger just above the water. Make sure the needle is parallel to the surface of the water, and then release the needle. If the needle sinks, dry it off completely and carefully try again until the needle floats.

results ☆   Surface tension is the pull of any liquid on its open surface so that the surface is as small as possible. The molecules near the surface pull on those that are on the surface. This pulling concentrates the molecules at the surface into a thin skin called *surface tension*. In the experiment, the water molecules near and on the surface press

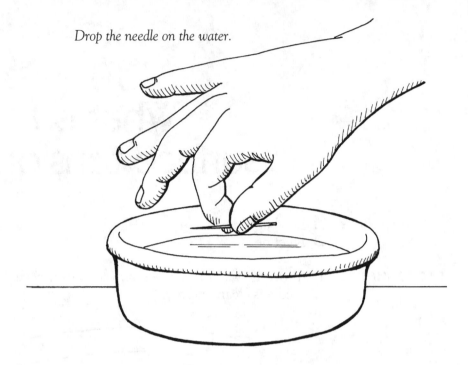

Drop the needle on the water.

together, forming the surface tension. The surface tension keeps the needle from sinking.

further ☆ **studies**
Look closely and you can see the surface film bending down under the weight of the needle. Have you seen dents in the surface when a spider walked on water? Pour a drop of liquid detergent into the bowl of water. Does the needle sink? Does detergent change the surface tension of water?

did you ☆ **know?**
❏ That soap bubbles are round because of surface tension. Soap reduces the water's surface tension and makes the water flexible enough to shape the bubble so that it takes up the least space.
❏ That if you hold a spoon under a stream of water, a round sheet of water—held together by surface tension—will form.
❏ That surface tension causes water to move through a cloth or paper towel.

31
What does air weigh?

materials ☆ ❑ Yardstick
❑ Two sheets of newspaper
❑ Worktable

procedure ☆ 1. Place the yardstick on the table with about 12 inches (30.48 cm) sticking over the edge. Push down abruptly on the free end of the yardstick.

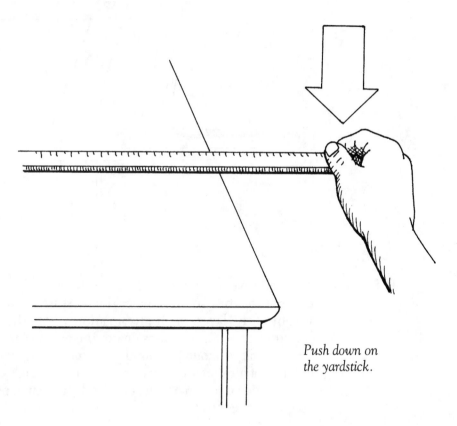

Push down on the yardstick.

2. Spread the sheets of newspaper over the yardstick and smooth them flat against the table. Now push down on the exposed end of the yardstick.

Smooth the paper and push down on the yardstick.

results ☆ Normally, we don't notice the pressure of air upon us, but air has a definite weight. *Air pressure*, or the pressure of air, is caused by the weight of the layers of air pressing down from the atmosphere. The pressure of the air increases nearer the earth. Air pressure at sea level averages about 15 pounds on every square inch. The tall column of air pressing down on you might weigh as much as 2,000 pounds. Because you are surrounded by an equal pressure of air, you do not feel the weight.

For example, imagine that you are walking on the ocean floor. You would not feel the extreme weight of the water above you because of the pressure of the water around you. Without the newspapers, very little effort is required to push down on the yardstick. But when the papers are spread over the yardstick, it hardly moved when you pushed down. The weight of the air on the newspaper kept the other end of the stick from rising.

further ☆ studies
Do you feel any air pressing down on you? Would you feel less pressure if you were under a table? Would a scuba diver feel less pressure swimming under a ledge than over it? Does gravity affect air pressure?

did you ☆ know?
❑ That in 1643 an Italian scientist named Evangelista Torricelli proved that air had weight and took up space. Before that some people thought that air was a spirit.
❑ That the temperature of the air normally decreases about 3 or 4 degrees for each 1,000 feet (305 meters) up from the earth.
❑ That the air in the average drinking glass weighs about the same as an aspirin tablet.

Evangelista Torricelli

32
What are sound waves?

materials ☆
- ❏ Empty round box with lid (salt or oat cereal box)
- ❏ Tape
- ❏ Candle mounted in metal lid
- ❏ Match

procedure ☆
1. If a salt box is used, ask an adult for help in removing the metal spout. If an oat box is used, have an adult cut a hole, about the size of a dime, in the center of the bottom of the box. Use tape to seal the top in place.

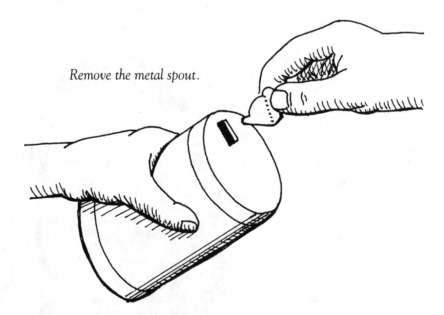

Remove the metal spout.

2. Ask an adult for permission to light a candle. Light the candle and, from 3 feet (about 1 meter) away, aim the hole in the box at the candle.
3. Sharply thump the other end of the box with your finger.

4. Move closer to the candle and thump the box, and then try it again farther from the box. Record the results to determine the range of the sound wave.

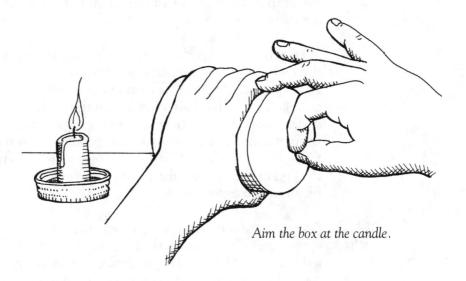

Aim the box at the candle.

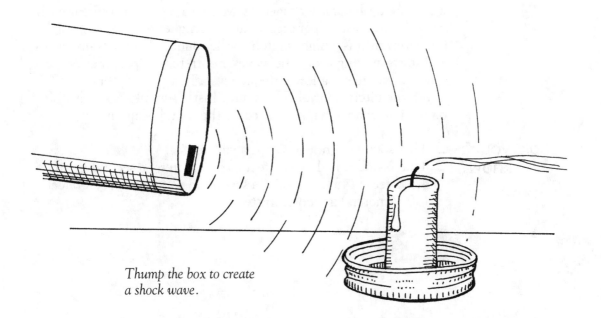

Thump the box to create a shock wave.

results ☆ All sounds have one thing in common. They are caused when something vibrates. When something vibrates, it causes the surrounding air to vibrate. As the air vibrates, it forms sound waves that travel out in all directions until the waves weaken and die away.

When the waves reach our ears, our eardrums vibrate and change the vibrations into sound. Sound travels in waves similar to the waves you see if you toss a rock in a pool of water. Small waves travel outward in all directions from the point where the rock strikes the surface of the water. In the experiment, you might have to try two or three times to adjust the aim, but you should be able to blow out the flame from several feet away. When you thumped the end of the box, it vibrated, sending out a sound wave that blew out the candle.

further ☆
studies Listen to the sound of a train or an emergency vehicle as it approaches. Then notice the sound as it moves away. Did you hear a difference? The *pitch*, or *frequency*, of a train whistle seems to sound higher as the train comes closer, then becomes lower as the source moves away. As the train or vehicle approaches, the sound waves are pushed closer together. More waves reach your ear each second. More waves per second mean a higher frequency. A higher frequency means a higher pitch to the sound. When a train passes and starts moving away, the waves are stretched apart. Fewer sound waves mean a lower frequency. When the frequency is lower, the pitch is lower. The train whistle actually has only one pitch. The change happens because the sound is moving.

did you ☆
know?
❑ That sound cannot travel in a vacuum.
❑ That sound travels 1,100 feet (335.5 meters) a second in air, 4,700 feet (1433.5 meters) a second in water, and 16,400 feet (5002 meters) a second in steel.

33
What bends light?

materials ☆
- ❏ Glue
- ❏ Sewing thread
- ❏ Dark solid-colored marble
- ❏ Flashlight
- ❏ Box support for flashlight
- ❏ Tape
- ❏ Sheet of white paper

procedure ☆ 1. Glue one end of the thread to the marble. While the glue is drying, place the flashlight on the box under the edge of a table or an open countertop.

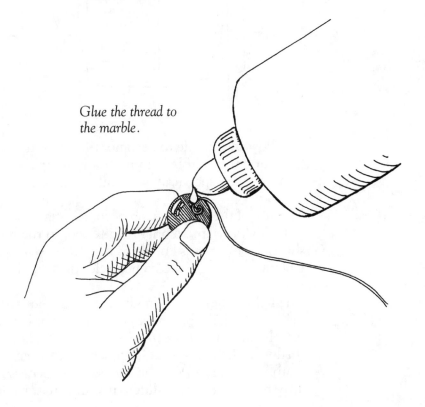

Glue the thread to the marble.

2. Turn on the flashlight. Use tape to suspend the marble on its thread from the edge of the table so that it is about 3 inches (7.62 cm) in front of, and exactly in line with, the beam of the flashlight.

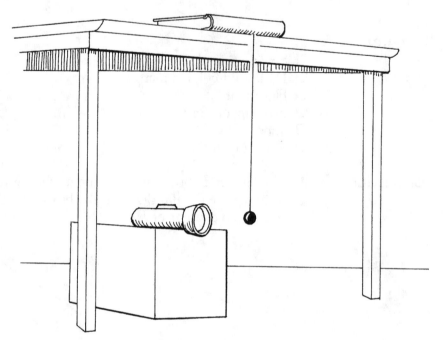

Suspend the marble in front of the flashlight.

3. Allow the marble to become still. Place the paper directly behind the marble to form a dark, sharp shadow. Now slowly move the paper away, gradually reducing the size of the shadow.

results ☆ The size of the shadow soon becomes a small, dark spot and then suddenly turns into a bright white spot in the middle of a gray shadow. This spot is known as the *Arago white spot*, after Dominique Arago, the French scientist who discovered it.

The light waves bend (are diffracted) as they pass the edge of the marble. As the paper moves back, the light bends around the marble until it forms a white spot in its shadow. The center of the shadow is the focusing point for the light from the edge of the marble. The rest of the shadow is darker because the light waves arriving there are bent differently and are traveling different

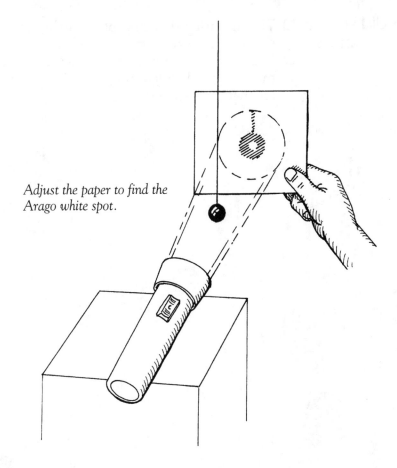

Adjust the paper to find the Arago white spot.

distances. These waves interfere with each other and are not in focus. *Diffracted* refers to light bending as it passes the edge of an object. *Refracted* refers to light bending as it passes through a substance.

further ☆ studies Place a coin at the inside edge of a bowl. Position your head so that you can only see the outer edge of the coin, and slowly add water to the bowl. Does the coin move into full view? Are light rays from the coin bent (refracted) as they pass through the water? Hold a piece of flat glass with drops of water on it over a sheet of white paper. What do the shadows look like? Raise and lower the glass. What happens to the shadows?

❏ That in earlier times, people thought that light was something that traveled from our eyes to what ever we saw.

❏ That in 1675 a Danish astronomer, Olaus Roemer, calculated that the speed of light was about 192,000 miles (308,928 kilometers) a second.

34
What causes
volcanoes to erupt?

materials ☆
- ❏ Drinking glass
- ❏ Vinegar
- ❏ Red food coloring
- ❏ Funnel
- ❏ Small plastic pop bottle
- ❏ Baking soda
- ❏ Large pan or tray
- ❏ Sand and gravel

procedure ☆
1. Fill the glass about half full of vinegar and add a few drops of food coloring.
2. Use the funnel to fill the pop bottle about half full of baking soda.
3. Stand the bottle in the tray and pile gravel and sand around the bottle to make a mountain.
4. Place the funnel in the bottle, and quickly pour in the red vinegar.

results ☆
Red "lava" pours out of your mountain in the form of an eruption because baking soda and vinegar react to form carbon dioxide gas. A real volcano is an opening in the earth's surface. Chambers of extremely hot *magma* (melted rock) lie miles below the base of the volcano. Magma contains gases made up mostly of steam. The gases are so hot that they exert a tremendous explosive pressure that sooner or later pushes through the weaker places in the earth's outer crust. A passage called a *vent*, or *conduit*, carries the explosive gases and rock to the earth's surface.

further studies ☆
Look at a map of the world and find some of the best known volcanoes. Look for the mid-Atlantic ridge. Was this ridge caused by volcanic action? What forces created Iceland? Can geothermal heat be used to heat homes and factories?

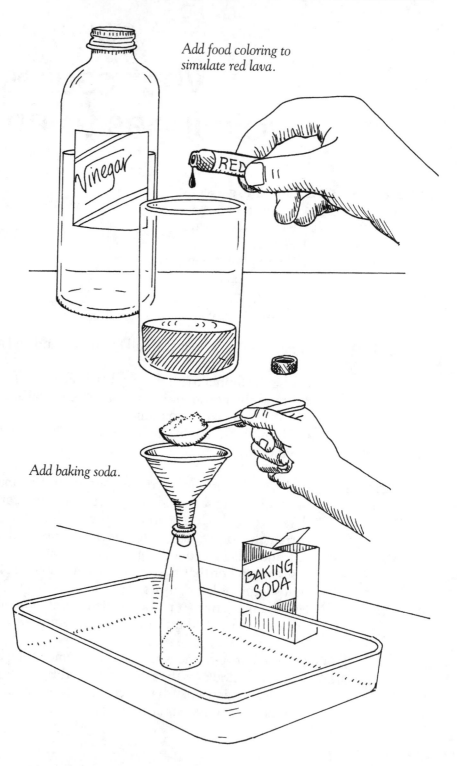

Add food coloring to simulate red lava.

Add baking soda.

The young physicist

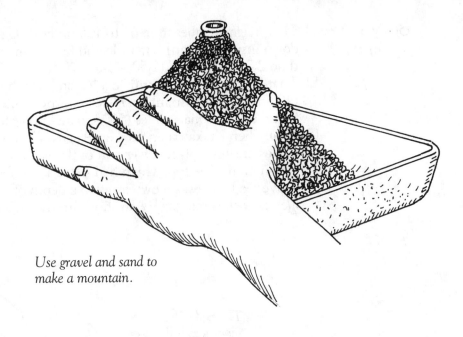

Use gravel and sand to make a mountain.

Quickly add vinegar.

❏ That magma comes from 62 to 125 miles (100 to 200 km) down inside the earth's mantle and has a temperature of more than 2,732 degrees F (1,500 C).

❏ That in May 1980, a terrific explosion blew the top 1,300 feet (400 meters) off Mount St. Helens in the United States and flattened 193 square miles (500 square km) of forest.

❏ That when Krakatoa erupted on August 27, 1883, four violent explosions took place. Over half of the island volcano was blown away. The top, which had stood 1,500 feet (457 meters) above sea level, was blown away to a depth of 1,000 feet (305 meters) below sea level. Ash shot into the air 17 miles (27.4

The explosions created shock waves that were heard as far as 3,000 miles (4,827 km) away.

km) and drifted around the earth. Some ash from Krakatoa even fell on western Europe 11,000 miles (17,699 km) away. The sound of the explosions were heard almost 3,000 miles (4,827 km) away.

Index

A

acids and bases experiments, 57-61, **58, 59, 60**
  acids in bee stings, 61
  acids in foods, 61
  household acids and bases, 61
  salts: combining acids and bases, 61
  using indicator strips, **60**, 61
action/reaction (Newton's third law of motion), 14-15
aerodynamics, Bernoulli principle, 5-6
air pressure experiments, 8-10, **8, 9**, 121-123, **121, 122**
  Bernoulli principle, 5-6
  changing air pressure, 122-123
  equatorial low-pressure area, Coriolis effect, 89
  hot air rises/cool air sinks, 64, 81, 84-85, 91, **91, 92**
  isobars, 90-91, **91**
  polar high-pressure area, Coriolis effect, 89
  rotation of high- and low-pressure areas, 92
  storms, 10
  temperature vs. height of air, 123
  tornadoes, 10
  Torricelli's experiments, 123
  underwater pressure, 123
  winds, 10
alchemists of the Middle Ages, 55
alternating current (ac), 26
altitude above horizon, 48, 50, **50**
anemometers, 79
Arago white spot, 128, **129**
Arago, Dominique, 128
arteries, 113, **114**, 115
astronomy, 37-53

Big Dipper, 44, **44**
calendars and astronomy, 37
distance from earth to sun, 44
distance from sun to nearest star, 44
earth-centered universe theories, 37
galaxies, 37-38
horizon experiment, 46-47, **46**
latitude experiment, 48-50, **49, 50**
Little Dipper, 44, **44**
magnetic vs. true north, 44
meridian experiment, 51-53, **51, 52**
Milky Way galaxy, 38
North Star photographs, 43-45, **44, 45**
solar system, 38
telescope to explore the universe, 37-38, **38**
twinkling star experiment, 39-42, 40, **41, 42**
atoms and atomic structures, 76

B

barometers, 79
bases (*see* acids and bases experiments)
Bernoulli principle of air pressure, 5-6
Bernoulli, Daniel, 5, **6**
bicycle gears, 18
Big Dipper, 44, **44**
biology, 99-115
  heart and circulation experiment, 112-115, **112, 113, 114**
  lungs and breathing experiment, 108-111, **109, 110**
  photosynthesis experiment, 101-104, **102, 103**

boldface page numbers indicate illustrations

biology, *cont.*
  tree rings and age of trees, 105-107, **105, 106**
Boone, Daniel, 102, **104**
breathing (*see* lungs and breathing experiment)

C

calendars and astronomy, 37
cambium layer of tree bark, 105-106
capillaries, 115
carbon dioxide experiment, 70, 72-74, **72, 73**
  animal life gives off carbon dioxide, 73
  breathing, carbon dioxide/oxygen exchange, 108, 110, 115
  carbonated beverages, 74
  density/weight of carbon dioxide, 74
  dry ice, 74
  plants, photosynthesis, and carbon dioxide, 73
carbon experiments, 69-71, **69, 70**
  carbon dioxide from burning carbon, 70
  carbon-14 to date fossils, 71
  diamonds as form of carbon, 71
  fuels containing carbon, 71
  hydrocarbons, 71
  sugar burning: carbon, hydrogen, oxygen produced, 70-71
carbon-14 to date fossils, 71
carbonated beverages, 74
cardiopulmonary resuscitation (CPR), 110
Cato the Elder, Marcus Porcius, 67, **67**
chemistry, 55-78
  acids and bases experiments, 57-61, **58, 59, 60**
  alchemists of the Middle Ages, 55
  carbon dioxide experiment, 72-74, **72, 73**
  carbon experiments, 69-71, **69, 70**
  fuels and energy research, 56
  ice floatation experiment, 62-64, **62, 63, 64**

  medical research, 55-56
  new materials from chemistry, 55
  starch experiment, 65-68, **65, 66**
  water composition experiment, 75-78, **76, 77, 78**
circulation (*see* heart and circulation experiment)
clouds experiment, 80-82, **80, 81, 82**
  condensation, 81
  cumulonimbus clouds, 82
  fog, 82
  height of clouds, 82
  hot air rises/cool air sinks, 81
  sailing and cloud observation, 82
  types of clouds, 81-82
conclusions in scientific method, vii
condensation, 81, 84-85
Coriolis force experiment, 87-89, **87, 88**
  equatorial calms, 89
  equatorial low pressure area, 89
  polar high pressure area, 89
  trade winds, 89
Coriolis, Gaspard G., 89
cumulonimbus clouds, 82

D

da Vinci, Leonardo, helicopter designs, 6
dew point experiment, 93-95, **93, 94**
  air conditioning vs. dew point, 95
  frost, 95
  humidity vs. dew point, 95
dextrin formed from starch, 67
diamonds as form of carbon, 71
diaphragm muscles, lungs and breathing, 108
diffraction (bending) of light, 128-129
direct current (dc), 26
dry ice, 74

E

earth as magnet, 31, **31**
earth-centered universe theories, 37
Edison, Thomas, 27, **27**
electrical circuit experiment, 24-27, **24, 25, 26**

1893 Chicago Exposition exhibit, 27
alternating current (ac), 26
appliance use, 26-27
current flow, 25-26, **26**
direct current (dc), 26
Edison's experiments, 27, **27**
filament in bulb, 25
heat vs. light from lightbulbs, 27
incandescent lights, 27
load, 25
electromagnetism experiment, 33-
    36, **33, 34, 35**
motors, 32
Oersted's experiments, 36
permanent magnet vs.
    electromagnet, 36
turns of wire vs. strength, 36
uses of electromagnets, 36
engineering, 1-36
  aeronautical engineering, 1
  air pressure experiments, 8-10, **8, 9**
  electrical circuit experiment, 24-
    27, **24, 25, 26**
  electromagnetism experiment, 33-
    36, **33, 34, 35**
  gears experiment, 16-18, **16, 17**
  magnetic fields experiment, 28-32,
    28, 29, 30, 31
  mechanical engineering, 1
  Panama Canal, 1
  paper airplane experiment, 3-7, **3,
    4, 5**
  pulleys experiment, 19-23, **19, 20,
    21, 22**
  Pyramids of Egypt, 1, **2**
  rocket experiment, 11-15, **11, 12,
    13, 14**
  San Francisco-Oakland Bay Bridge,
    1, **2**
  types of engineers, 1
equatorial calms, 89
experiments, vii

F
fog, 82
fossils, carbon-14 to date fossils, 71
frequency of sound, 126
fronts in weather, 90-92, **90, 91, 92**

equatorial low-pressure area,
    Coriolis effect, 89
hot air rises/cool air sinks, 91, **91,
    92**
hurricanes, 92
isobars, 90-91, **90**
polar high-pressure area, Coriolis
    effect, 89
rotation of high- and low-pressure
    areas, 92
storms and fronts, 91
tornadoes, 92
weather associated with different
    fronts, 91
winds and isobars, 91
frost, 95

G
galaxies, 37-38
  Milky Way, 38
gears experiment, 16-18, **16, 17**
  bicycle gears, 18
  water wheels, 18
geothermal heat sources, 131
Gilbert, William, 31
gliders and sailplanes, 6

H
hail (*see* rain, snow, hail experiment)
heart and circulation experiment,
    112-115, **112, 113, 114**
  beats per minute, 115
  capillaries, 115
  carbon dioxide/oxygen exchange,
    115
  length of blood vessels in body, 115
  pulse counting, 113
  stethoscope construction, 112
  strength of heart muscle, 115
  veins and arteries, 113, **114**, 115
  volume of blood pumped, 115
Heimlich maneuver, 110
helicopter, Leonardo da Vinci
    design, 6
horizon experiment, 46-47, **46**
  altitude above horizon, 48, 50, **50**
  distance to horizon, land vs. sea vs.
    air, 47

relative size of Moon vs. horizon, 47
humidity in air, 76
  dew point, 95
hurricanes, 92
hydrogen, 70, 75
hygrometers, 79
hypothesis formation in scientific method, vii

I

ice floatation experiment, 62-64, **62, 63, 64**
  force of expanding ice, 64
  gravity's force on ice and water, 63-64
  hot air rises/cool air sinks, 64
  marine life and ice, 64
  molecular structure of ice, 63-64
incandescent lights, 27
international date line, 53
interpreting data, vii
iodine to test for starch, 66, **66**
isobars, 90-91, **90**

K

Key, Francis Scott, 15
Krakatoa volcanic eruption (1883), 132, **134**

L

latitude experiment, 48-50, **49, 50**
  altitude above horizon, 48, 50, **50**
  degrees of measurement, 48
  minutes and seconds of latitude, 50
  time measured from altitude/latitude, 50
lava, 131
light experiments, 127-130, **127, 128, 129**
  Arago white spot, 128, **129**
  diffraction (bending) of light, 128-129
  early theories about light, 130
  mirages, 40
  prisms, 97
  rainbow experiment, 96-98, **96, 97**

refraction of light, 40, 129
  shadows, 129
  speed of light, 130
Little Dipper, 44, **44**
longitude determination, 52-53
lungs and breathing experiment, 108-111, **109, 110**
  air pollution, 110
  air sacs in lungs, 108, 111
  carbon dioxide/oxygen exchange, 108, 110, 115
  cardiopulmonary resuscitation (CPR), 110
  circulation of blood through lungs, 108, 115
  diaphragm muscles, 108
  elasticity of lungs, 111
  Heimlich maneuver, 110
  size and weight of lungs, 111

M

magma, 131, 132
magnetic fields experiment, 28-32, **28, 29, 30, 31**
  cutting a magnet, 32
  discovery of earth as magnet, 31, **31**
  electric motors, 32
  electricity and magnetic fields, 32
  electromagnetism, 32
  magnetic pole of earth, 31, **31**
  magnetic vs. true north, 44
  migration of birds and whales, 32
marine life and ice, 64
mechanical advantage, pulleys, 21-22, 23
meridian experiment, 51-53, **51, 52**
  distance between meridians, 53
  international date line, 53
  longitude determination, 52
  prime meridian at Greenwich, England, 52
  time zones, 53
meteorology, 79-98
  anemometers, 79
  barometers, 79
  clouds experiment, 80-82, **80, 81, 82**

Coriolis force experiment, 87-89, **87, 88**
dew point experiment, 93-95, **93, 94**
droughts, 85
economic impact of weather, 79
floods, 85
forecasting the weather, 79
fronts in weather, 90-92, **90, 91, 92**
frost, 95
humidity in the air, 76
hurricanes, 92
hygrometers, 79
rain, snow, hail experiment, 83-86, **83, 84, 85**
rainbow experiment, 96-98, **96, 97**
space shuttle launches vs. weather, 79, **79**
thermometers, 79
tornadoes, 92
migration of animals and earth's magnetic field, 32
Milky Way galaxy, 38
mirages, 40
motion, Newton's third law of motion: action/reaction, 14-15
motors, electric motors and magnets, 32
Mount St. Helens volcanic eruption (1980), 132

N
Newton's third law of motion: action/reaction, 14-15
Newton, Isaac, **14**
North Star photographs, 43-45, **44, 45**

O
Oersted, Hans Christian, 36
oxygen, 70, 75
  breathing, carbon dioxide/oxygen exchange, 108, 110, 115

P
Panama Canal, 1
paper airplane experiment, 3-7, 3, **4, 5**

Bernoulli principle, 5-6
  gliders and sailplanes, 6
  helicopter designed by da Vinci, 6
  space shuttle design, 6
  Wright brothers' earliest attempts, 6, **7**
phloem layer of tree bark, 106
photographic projects, North Star photographs, 43-45, **44, 45**
photosynthesis, 73, 101-104, **102, 103**
  chlorophyll, 101
  mushrooms and photosynthesis, 101
physics, 117-135
  air pressure experiment, 121-123, **121, 122**
  light experiment, 127-130, 127, **128, 129**
  sound waves experiment, 124-126, **124, 125**
  surface tension experiment, 119-120, **119, 120**
  volcanic eruptions, 131-135, **132, 133, 134, 135**
pitch of sounds, 126
plants
  carbon dioxide and photosynthesis, 73
  chlorophyll, 101
  movement of plants, 101
  mushrooms and photosynthesis, 101
  photosynthesis, 73, 101-104, **102, 103**
  poisonous plants, 102
  starch in plants and plant materials, 67-68
  tree rings and age of trees, 105-107, **105, 106**
poisonous plants, 102
poles, North and South poles of earth, 31, **31**
  magnetic vs. true north, 44
prime meridian at Greenwich, England, 52-53
prisms, 97

problem-stating in scientific
   method, vii
pulleys experiment, 19-23, **19, 20,**
   21, 22
  double block and tackle, 23
  fixed pulleys, 20, **20**
  mechanical advantage, 21-22, 23
  movable pulleys, 20, **21**
  single block and tackle, 21, **22**
Pyramids of Egypt, 1, **2**

R
rain, snow, hail experiment, 83-86,
   83, 84, 85
  condensation, 84-85
  fish and frogs in rain, 86
  floods vs. droughts, 85
  hot air rises/cool air sinks, 84-85
  rainforests, annual rainfall, 85
  shape of raindrops, 86
rainbow experiment, 96-98, **96, 97**
  colors of rainbow, 97
  duration of rainbows, 98
  height of rainbow, 97
  moon rainbows, 98
  prism formation, 97
  rainbows observed from airplanes, 98
rainforests and annual rainfall, 85
refraction of light, 40, 129
rocket experiment, 11-15, **11, 12,**
   13, 14
  Chinese invention of rockets, 15
  Newton's third law of motion:
   action/reaction, 14-15
  The Star-Spangled Banner's "rockets'
   red glare," 15
  warfare and rockets, 15
Roemer, Olaus, 130

S
salts, combining acids and bases, 61
San Francisco-Oakland Bay Bridge,
   1, **2**
scientific method, vii
shadows, 129
snow (*see* rain, snow, hail
   experiment)
soap vs. surface tension, 120

solar system, 38
sound waves experiment, 124-126,
   124, 125
  frequency, 126
  pitch, 126
  speed of sound, 126
  vibrations and sound, 126
space shuttle, 79, **79**
  aerodynamic design of shuttle, 6
  weather conditions vs. launches, 79
starch experiment, 65-68, **65, 66**
  chlorophyllic plants and starch, 68
  common objects containing starch,
   67
  dextrin formed from starch, 67
  early uses of starch, 67-68
  iodine to test for starch, 66, **66**
stars (*see* astronomy; twinkling star
   experiment)
The Star-Spangled Banner's "rockets'
   red glare," 15
stethoscope construction, 112
storms, 10
  weather fronts and storms, 91
sugars, dextrin formed from starch,
   67
surface tension experiment, 119-120,
   119, 120
  soap vs. surface tension, 120
symbols used in book, ix

T
telescope to explore the universe,
   37-38, **38**
Tesla, Nikola, 27, **27**
thermometers, 79
time measured from altitude/latitude,
   50
time zones, 53
tornadoes, 10, 92
Torricelli, Evangelista, 123
trade winds, 89
tree rings and age of trees, 105-107,
   105, 106
  biggest trees on earth, 107
  cambium layer, 105-106
  growth of trees, 107
  oldest trees on earth, 107

phloem layer, 106
weather vs. tree growth, 106
twinkling star experiment, 39-42,
    40, 41, 42
  heat and air density, 39-40
  mirages, 40
  refraction of light, 40

V

veins, 113, **114**, 115
vents or conduits in volcanoes, 131
vibrations and sound, 126
volcanic eruptions, 131-135, **132,
    133, 134, 135**
  geothermal heat sources, 131
  Krakatoa eruption (1883), 132, **134**
  lava, 131
  location of volcanoes on earth, 131
  magma, 131, 132
  Mount St. Helens eruption (1980),
    132
  vents or conduits in volcanoes, 131

W

water composition experiment
  amount of water needed per day,
    76
  amount of water on earth, 77
  atomic structure of water, 76
  composition of water experiment,
    75-78, **76, 77, 78**
  condensation, 81, 84-85
  humidity in the air, 76
  hydrogen in water, 75
  oxygen in water, 75
  recycling of water on earth, 77
  surface tension experiment, 119-
    120, **119, 120**
water wheels and gears, 18
Westinghouse, George, 27
winds, 10
  equatorial calms, 89
  isobars and wind speeds, 91
  trade winds, 89
Wright brothers, 6, **7**

About the Author

Robert W. Wood has professional experience in aviation science, experimental agriculture, electricity, electronics, and science research. He is the author of more than a dozen physics and science books, as well as several home maintenance books. His work has been featured in major newspapers and magazines, and he has been a guest on radio talk shows around the United States. Some of his books have been translated into other languages, including Turkish.

Bob enjoys the wonders of nature and is always interested in the advances of science and how it affects our lifestyles. Although he has traveled and worked worldwide, he now lives with his wife and family in Arizona.

Other Bestsellers
of Related Interest

How? More Experiments for the Young Scientist
—Dave Prochnow and Kathy Prochnow
Provides more than 40 illustrated experiments in astronomy, aerodynamics, engineering, life sciences, chemistry, meteorology, and physics—for children ages 8-13. Each a self-contained lesson focusing on a specific natural or man-made occurrence, these projects teach children important learning skills like following directions, observing carefully, and accurately recording information.
ISBN 0-8306-4025-8 $9.95 Paper
ISBN 0-8306-4024-X $16.95 Hard

Why? 49 Experiments for the Young Scientist
—Dave and Kathy Prochnow
For kids ages 8 to 13, this project book answers 49 of the most frequently asked "why?" questions children ask about science. These fun, simple, safe, and inexpensive experiments satisfy a child's natural curiosity about science by clearly demonstrating specific scientific principles and explaining how they affect us in our daily lives. Topics include engineering, astronomy, chemistry, meteorology, biology, and physics.
ISBN 0-8306-4023-1 $9.95 Paper
ISBN 0-8306-4015-0 $16.95 Hard

Toys in Space: Exploring Science with the Astronauts
—Dr. Carolyn Sumners
An unparalleled resource for elementary and middle-school science teachers and parents. Contains dozens of toy-building activities that simulate experiments NASA astronauts perform on space missions, teaching children the principles of physics through play.
ISBN 0-8306-4534-9 $10.95 Paper
ISBN 0-8306-4533-0 $17.95 Hard

Science For Kids: 39 Easy Astronomy Experiments
—*Robert W. Wood*

These safe and fun experiments introduce kids ages 8-13 to the wonders of the sky. Experimenters learn to tell time by the sun, make maps of the stars and constellations, and much more.

ISBN 0-8306-3597-1 $9.95 Paper

Science For Kids: 39 Easy Chemistry Experiments
—*Robert W. Wood*

Grades 3-9. A gold mine of fun ideas for science educators, parents, scout leaders, and kids. Using safe, inexpensive materials, these innovative, quick experiments allow children to grow a crystal garden, soften water, test for starch in foods, and more.

ISBN 0-8306-3596-3 $9.95 Paper
ISBN 0-8306-7596-5 $17.95 Hard

Environmental Science: High School Science Fair Experiments—*H. Steven Dashefsky*

Students learn about an environment in crisis with hands-on science projects. Covers the biosphere, atmosphere, soil and aquatic ecology, energy sources, and applied ecology.

ISBN 0-8306-4586-1 $12.95 Paper
ISBN 0-8306-4587-X $19.95 Hard

Space and Astronomy: 49 Science Fair Projects
—*Robert L. Bonnet and G. Daniel Keen*

To celebrate The International Space Year in 1992, this exciting collection of science fair projects introduces young experimenters to the fundamentals of aeronautics and space science. Students explore such topics as comprehending astronomical numbers, determining the size of a meteorite, using falling sand as a time keeper, proving the earth is round, tracking comets, identifying stars, comparing, the characteristics of different planets, and more.

ISBN 0-8306-3938-1 $9.95 Paper
ISBN 0-8306-3939-X $16.95 Hard

How to Order

 Call 1-800-822-8158
24 hours a day,
7 days a week
in U.S. and Canada

 Mail this coupon to:
McGraw-Hill, Inc.
Blue Ridge Summit, PA
17294-0840

 Fax your order to:
717-794-5291

 EMAIL
70007.1531@COMPUSERVE.COM
COMPUSERVE: GO MH

Thank you for your order!

Shipping and Handling Charges

Order Amount	Within U.S.	Outside U.S.
Less than $15	$3.45	$5.25
$15.00 - $24.99	$3.95	$5.95
$25.00 - $49.99	$4.95	$6.95
$50.00 - and up	$5.95	$7.95

EASY ORDER FORM—
SATISFACTION GUARANTEED

Ship to:

Name _____

Address _____

City/State/Zip _____

Daytime Telephone No. _____

ITEM NO.	QUANTITY	AMT.

Method of Payment:

☐ Check or money order enclosed (payable to McGraw-Hill)

☐ Cards ☐ *VISA*

☐ MasterCard ☐ DISCOVER

Shipping & Handling charge from chart below	
Subtotal	
Please add applicable state & local sales tax	
TOTAL	

Account No. □□□□□□□□□□□□□□□

Signature _____ Exp. Date _____
Order invalid without signature

**In a hurry? Call 1-800-822-8158 anytime,
day or night, or visit your local bookstore.**

Code = BC44ZNA